INTERNATIONAL
RELATIONS
ALL THAT MATTERS

INTERNATIONAL RELATIONS

Ken Booth

First published in Great Britain in 2014 by Hodder & Stoughton. An Hachette UK company.

First published in US in 2014 by The McGraw-Hill Companies, Inc.

This edition published 2014

British Library Cataloguing in Publication Data: a catalogue record for this title is available from the British Library.

Library of Congress Catalog Card Number: on file.

10 9 8 7 6 5 4 3 2 1

Paperback ISBN 978 1 444 19001 4

eBook ISBN 978 1 444 19003 8

The publisher has used its best endeavours to ensure that any website addresses referred to in this book are correct and active at the time of going to press. However, the publisher and the author have no responsibility for the websites and can make no guarantee that a site will remain live or that the content will remain relevant, decent or appropriate.

The publisher has made every effort to mark as such all words which it believes to be trademarks. The publisher should also like to make it clear that the presence of a word in the book, whether marked or unmarked, in no way affects its legal status as a trademark.

Every reasonable effort has been made by the publisher to trace the copyright holders of material in this book. Any errors or omissions should be notified in writing to the publisher, who will endeavour to rectify the situation for any reprints and future editions.

Typeset by Cenveo® Publisher Services.

Printed and bound in Great Britain by CPI Group (UK) Ltd., Croydon, CRO 4YY.

John Murray Learning policy is to use papers that are natural, renewable and recyclable products and made from wood grown in sustainable forests. The logging and manufacturing processes are expected to conform to the environmental regulations of the country of origin.

John Murray Learning

338 Euston Road

London NW1 3BH

www.hodder.co.uk

Thanks are due to Eurwen Booth, Tim Dunne, Jan Ruzicka, Kamila Stullerova and Nicholas J. Wheeler for their good advice; they bear no responsibility for the book's failings.

About the author

Ken Booth is an academic who has given presentations in some 30 countries and whose work has been translated into ten languages. He has published nearly 30 books, as well as numerous articles and chapters. He is a Fellow of the British Academy (FBA) and a recipient of the International Studies Association's Susan Strange Award in recognition of his contribution to challenging conventional wisdom and intellectual complacency in the international studies community. He is presently Senior Research Associate in the Department of International Politics, Aberystwyth University, and president of the David Davies Memorial Institute of International Studies. He has been editor of the journal *International Relations* for over ten years and is a former chair of the British International Studies Association. A distinguished US scholar commented on his *Theory of World Security* (2007): 'If Nobel Prizes were given in international relations, Ken Booth would deserve one for this extraordinary book.'

Contents

1 Understanding the world   1

2 Anarchy, system, states   15

3 Theories, concepts, debates   31

4 Fear, power, security   47

5 Conflict, co-operation, statecraft   63

6 Political economy, capitalism, globalization   83

7 Values, ethics, choices   99

8 Inventing humanity   117

100 ideas   137

Index   149

1

Understanding the world

'We have learned that man's head, as a source of reality, is a strange and dangerous place.'

Philip Allott

This is a short book about the biggest questions in politics. By its end, no reader should be in doubt about the profound significance of international relations. I will show how the practices of international relations critically shape *who gets what* and *who is who* across the world, and how its theories inform *how we live together globally*, either in co-operation or in conflict. To paraphrase a famous dictum of Trotsky: you might not be interested (yet!) in international relations, but international relations are always interested in you.

▶ Why international relations matter

International relations matter for three broad sets of reasons: first, because much of what happens in the daily lives of everybody across the world is directly and indirectly the result of actually practised international relations in the past, at present, and (through informed and uninformed expectations) into the future; second, because dominant ideas about international relations shape the common sense of political elites about co-operation and conflict between human societies; and third, because the study of International Relations grapples with the most basic philosophical questions – What is real? What can we know? How should we live? – in the biggest political arena of all, the international system. As is conventional, from hereon 'IR' – capitalized and abbreviated – will be used to refer to the academic study of what takes place in the real world of 'international relations' – lower case – such as diplomacy, trade and military strategy.

Anarchy is the condition that defines the international system. According to Kenneth N. Waltz, the most influential theorist in IR since the Second World War, *anarchy* has enormous 'causal weight' (the power to make things happen) in relation to 'big and important things'. Other factors affect how 'the games of nations' are played – misperceptions, gender and race, for example – but the international political arena takes its basic character from the condition of anarchy.

Anarchy

Anarchy is used by IR specialists to refer to the situation in which there is no supreme political authority above the sovereign state. Anarchy in this technical sense does not necessarily imply 'chaos', 'disorder' and 'confusion' as it does in everyday usage: in international relations, anarchy can be a condition of order and stability. Anarchy does imply, however, that the states making up the international system must operate according to 'self-help' principles. With no higher power on which to rely, each state must look after its own security and wellbeing. It is the interaction of self-help units, states, that gives anarchy its 'causal weight'.

The 'big and important things' that Waltz claimed were explained by anarchy include war and peace, balances and imbalances of power, and structures of co-operation and domination. Over the centuries, these have been critical in shaping much of today's political world. They have helped construct which states are powerful and which have to bend the knee; which nations are richer and which poorer; where state boundaries have settled (or not); which peoples have productive land and which lands are barren; which have plentiful energy resources and which are dependent; and on and on. Political units everywhere, to greater or lesser degrees, are the products or playthings, winners or losers, victims or survivors of the self-help imperative of international relations over time. Much of what we take for granted in the daily activities of life on earth today is the result of battles and deals between states long, or not so long, ago. What's past in international relations is very present.

But Waltz's argument does not go deeply enough. The 'causal weight' of international structures, without doubt, helps explain *big and important* matters, but they in turn help explain *small and important things*, like who you are and who I am. This is because aspects of our personal lives were shaped, long before we were born, by the great tides of international relations. To put it simply, each of us is born into a specific national context, with a particular history, geography, culture and set of opportunities and constraints in the international system. As individuals or families, we may be able to change our national context, but this only underlines how much the conditions of possibility in our personal lives are set by the context of international relations. A person's relative wellbeing is directly affected by that context, as are such individual matters as one's sense of identity, the language one speaks, or the God one broadly worships (or not). Even the music one enjoys, certainly the national sporting teams one supports, are likely to be directly related to one's location on a map produced by international relations. Our thoughtways, which are shaped by the culture into which we were socialized (and which we probably celebrate 'with pride'), are the outcome of the power-plays of states in the near or distant past. If you doubt this, think for a moment about how your biography would have been different had you been born the other side of your nearest state border, never mind halfway across the world.

The ebb and flow of international relations take various forms. Major wars have particular transformative power. The Great War of 1914–18 decisively altered private and public lives in much of the world up to the present, the Second World War even more so. In both cases, inventions were accelerated, boundaries changed, political horizons altered, social dreams inspired, cultures destroyed, and, of course, lives and loves were changed for ever. More recently, the Cold War dominated the global political scene and drove the economic as well as the military policies of the protagonists. It affected everything from consumerism to culture to living with the nightmare possibility of nuclear annihilation. Far from the superpower eyeball-to-eyeball confrontation, bloody (proxy) wars were fought throughout this misnamed 'Long Peace'. Depending on one's specific Cold War location, mindsets and routines intruded into private lives through the demands of governments and the imagery of global enmity. The Cold War's shadow still stretches over the lives of people, places and politics in some parts of the world (as was clearly and dangerously the case as the crisis in the Ukraine deepened during the winter of 2013–14). The realities of the 'Global War on Terror' continue to have impact – even if its most inflammatory language has been abandoned – through military interventions and expansive routines of surveillance and control.

It is not my claim in this book that international relations determine every detail of the lives of everyone on earth, but it is my claim that international relations are of decisive significance. Consider, for example, the intrusive impact of European imperialism in previous centuries on the personal biographies, outlooks and opportunities of people today living in the Global South.

Each of us, as individuals, is shaped by our genetic inheritance, and the life chances created by our parents and their class, *but who we are* is inescapably related to specific geopolitical histories and geographies. Our lives, to some degree, take place in a context constructed by how well or badly particular governments in the past conducted themselves. We are all, whether we recognize it or not, the children of international relations.

▶ Accentuating the international

The word 'international' is a relatively recent historical invention. It is usually identified with the philosopher Jeremy Bentham, who in 1780 coined the term 'international' in his book *Introduction to the Principles of Morals and Legislation,* to describe the system of law between sovereign states. As a specific academic 'discipline', however, the term 'International Relations' is even more recent, dating from only 1919.

Scholars love to debate the definition of their discipline. This is hardly surprising, as there is always a great deal riding on where one draws the line between what is in or out. In this book, 'international relations' is defined simply as *the international level of world politics.* By 'international level' I mean the interactions largely (but not exclusively) of sovereign states; by 'world politics' I mean 'who gets what, when and how across the world', to stretch Harold Lasswell's classical definition of 'politics'.

The reason for accentuating the *international* level of world politics is twofold. First, as already mentioned, the international is a level with enormous 'causal weight'. Second, to engage with 'who gets what, when and how across the world' without a coherent focus such as 'the international level' is to invite bewilderment in the face of information overload. This problem is evident in many of the doorstep-sized textbooks about 'world' or 'global' politics: what in the world is not a matter of 'world politics'? The formulation proposed offers a distinct focus ('the international'), while being empirically open ('the world'). I owe this way of thinking largely to C.A.W. Manning, an early doyen of IR, who described academic international relations as having 'a focus but not a periphery'.

By focusing on the international, critics will say that I have succumbed to a 'state-centric' view of the world.

This is the idea that states are the fundamental reality of world politics. Such a view is sometimes also described as being 'statist', meaning endorsing the idea that the state is and should be the highest level of both political decision-making and loyalty. My position is more complicated: I want to recognize the empirical significance of states and their relations without being statist politically or ethically. This is like an atheist arguing about 'religion'. An atheist cannot for long discuss religion without talking about God, but this does not make the atheist 'God-centric'; it only means that the atheist is aware of the significance of God when talking about religion.

The book will argue that the international level of world politics is state-*dominated* in an empirical sense (some states are the most powerful 'actors' in the world) without succumbing to state-*centrism* in a normative sense (believing that the contemporary states-system represents the best of all possible worlds). Later chapters will underline that states are not the only actors at the international level: some multinational corporations have more clout than some states. Nonetheless, it would be foolish to play down the continuing significance of especially the most powerful states in determining 'who gets what' across the world, or the continuing 'causal weight' of state interactions in shaping the 'when and how' of things happening. Recognizing these empirical realities is perfectly consistent with accepting that one of the aims of studying IR is to challenge what is done, and why, and consider whether different worlds are possible and desirable.

The 'texture' of the international

We can get inside the mindset of the characters in Shakespeare's plays, appreciating Hamlet's indecision and Macbeth's ambition. Similarly, we can understand old dramas and dilemmas in international politics. When we think of the struggle for control of the 'Holy Land' between Israelis and Palestinians, we might recall Francis I of France, in the early fifteenth century, when he was asked what differences accounted for the constant wars between himself and Charles V, the Holy Roman Emperor. He supposedly replied: 'None whatever. We agree perfectly. We both want control of Italy.' Likewise, those in Europe who worry about Germany's domination of the eurozone will understand the view of European leaders at the end of the Thirty Years War in 1648 who were determined to keep the German lands broken up in the interests of the European balance of power; and they will appreciate the remark ascribed to a French diplomat at the end of the Second World War almost exactly 300 years later, who said, 'I love Germany so much, that's why I want two of them.' Size matters in international relations.

Matters of continuity and change are always present in international relations. According to the 'realist' tradition (explained later), the international level or system has had, again in Waltz's term, a distinct 'texture' (a persisting set of characteristics) over the centuries. This continuity allows us to have a time-transcending understanding of the situations, dilemmas and crises faced by leaders and peoples in other places in other eras. Critics of this view – those dazzled by what's new – tend to argue that talk of 'texture' exaggerates continuity. This is mistaken. There can be no doubt that we live in a new era when it comes to technology and its potential, for example, but have relations between political units fundamentally changed? We cannot, and should not, assume that everything will always be the same, but it would be foolish to underestimate the stubborn continuities of state interactions.

▶ Studying IR

The theme of this book is the profound reality of international relations in the life of the world – all the way down. Recognition of this was present at the very birth of the academic project of IR. The midwife was not academic enquiry for its own sake, but the political volcano and human catastrophe of 1914–18. The historian A.J.P. Taylor's verdict on the Great War was that nations fumbled into it 'more or less helplessly', and that 'The Unknown Soldier was the hero'. There was a desperate cry of 'Never again!' The world had to do better, and better knowledge about international relations was thought to be one way ahead.

As the following box on the IR canon shows, thinkers had been writing for millennia about peace and war between political units. Institutionally speaking, however, the study of IR was born in 1919 when David Davies – philanthropist, Liberal MP in Wales, 'peacemonger' and somebody who had seen action on the Western Front – endowed a Chair as a memorial to the students of the University College of Wales, Aberystwyth, who had fought and died in the conflict. From the beginning, Davies conceived the new field of study (which he called 'International Politics') in the broadest terms, proposing a syllabus that included, in addition to politics, the study of law, ethics, economics and different civilizations. Students of this new subject were challenged, as they still are, to have a remarkable and cross-disciplinary knowledge about how human society works globally. Integral to the project was a general commitment to understanding international politics in order to try and avoid the mistakes of the past. For almost all the early students in the discipline, with the millions of ghosts of the Great War on their shoulders, this meant managing and preferably abolishing the institution of war.

In the 1920s new Chairs of International Relations and academic centres quickly developed at Oxford, the London School of Economics and the Royal Institute of International Affairs ('Chatham House'). The subject also took root in the United States, and by the 1930s US universities (Chicago, Harvard, Yale) and research centres had established a domination that continues to the present day. In the interwar years, IR was very much a minority interest, but this changed radically with the 'Devil's Decade' of the 1930s being quickly followed by a second (and even more destructive) world war, the nuclear weapons revolution, and the global spread of the US–Soviet Cold War. The academic significance of IR grew, as did its popularity among students; and so it continues.

The historic IR canon

A cursory survey of the historic literature of those who have written about conflict and co-operation between city-states, empires and their colonies, civilizations, dynasties or modern states, would include writings on:

- war in ancient Greece (by Thucydides and Aristotle) and in China (by Mencius and Sun Tzu)

- the interests of states in the Middle Ages in the Middle East (by Ibn Khaldun) and South Asia (by Kautilya)

- the just war and other duties of states (by Thomas Aquinas, Francisco de Vitoria and Hugo Grotius)

- human nature and conflict (by Thomas Hobbes and Jean-Jacques Rousseau)

- using state power (by Niccolò Machiavelli and Friedrich Meinecke)

- the material foundations of politics (by Karl Marx, Friedrich Engels and Karl Kautsky)

- geopolitics (by Alfred Thayer Mahan and Harold J. Mackinder)

- military strategy (by Karl von Clausewitz and Colmar Freiherr von der Goltz)

- imperialism and colonialism (by John A. Hobson and Vladimir Illyich Lenin)

- the prospects for peace (by Erasmus and Immanuel Kant)

- the balance of power (by Emerich de Vattell and Friedrich von Gentz).

This is the historic IR canon, and, to a man, all men.

The United States remains the research and teaching superpower in IR, but in the 1960s the discipline spread throughout the English-speaking world and Western Europe. Since the 1980s IR has gone global. This 'worlding' of IR, as it is sometimes called, is of undoubted significance, but so far – and into the foreseeable future – the United States will remain the loudest voice; and English will continue to be the discipline's *lingua franca*, even if it does not have all the words. In the decades ahead, one of the most exciting developments will be watching to see whether globalized IR can produce any fundamentally new ideas about the character and potentials of the international level of world politics, or whether it will simply give different perspectives on old themes. Whatever the answer, the continuing drive for understanding, in the hope of better practice and outcomes, is a testament to the spreading recognition of how much international relations really matter.

2

Anarchy, system, states

'Our view of possible alternatives to the states system should take into account the limitations of our own imagination and our own inability to transcend past experience.'

Hedley Bull

We are often led to believe that *what is* was always *meant to be*. Certain things become seen as part of a grand plan, guided by Nature, God, Reason – or whatever. This way of thinking is called 'teleology', from the Greek word *telos* meaning 'purpose' or 'goal'. In the mid-eighteenth century the philosopher Voltaire satirized the holding of such views by describing a character who believed that the human nose had been designed in order that we could comfortably wear spectacles. Behind everything there must be an ultimate purpose. Today's nation-based patchwork of sovereign states – the international system – is commonly understood this way, as the natural or rational outcome for organizing the politics of human society globally. This chapter will question teleological temptations.

▶ 'We have worlds inside us'

Today's political map of the world – a pattern of 196 differently shaped and sized states – is normalized in our collective mind. It is the result, obviously, of long and complex historical processes; less obviously perhaps, it did not have to happen in the way or direction it did.

Human forms of identification, association and loyalty have altered radically through the millennia. People in the past, and some today, identified first with their village or tribe or religion before they identified with a particular 'nation-state', today's dominant and domineering marker of political identity. Human identities, associations and loyalties are *historical* not *natural* phenomena, and hence the title of this section, which comes from a painting by Edvard Munch. If we have 'worlds inside us', rather than being the playthings of a grand plan, how did today's political map of the world come about, with the sovereign state as its primary organizing device? 'We are as we are because we got that way' was the answer of the peace researcher Kenneth Boulding. It is a messy story

What is a state?

The basic international legal definition of a state was formulated in the Montevideo Convention of 1933. A state should have (i) a permanent population; (ii) a defined territory; (iii) a government; and (iv) the capacity to enter into relations with other states. Some have criticized this formulation because it does not include the criterion of formal 'recognition', according to which a state is not a 'legal person' until it has been acknowledged as such by other states.

The political organization of human society globally need not have taken the course it did. According to the sociologist Mike Featherstone, alternative trajectories included: the global hegemony of one power (a world state under one overall ruler); a global federal system (a decentralized world state); the triumph of one dominant religion and its related political and theocratic structures; or the communist vision of a system dominated by the universal proletariat. Other possible trajectories include a world comprised of empires, or city-states, or tribes, or civilizations. In an influential but highly controversial book (*The Clash of Civilizations and the Remaking of World*

Order, published in 1996), political scientist Samuel P. Huntington asserted that it is not states (legal entities) but civilizations (cultural entities) that represent the most fundamental building blocks of human life. The puzzle to be addressed in this chapter is how multiple possible forms of political identity, association and loyalty developed in the direction they did, leading to the triumph in recent centuries of the sovereign nation-state system.

Thinking as historians, we must be careful to avoid simply reading history backwards, believing that what happened was inevitable. The past was more open than it now appears, and what presently exists, and seems natural and normal, arrived relatively recently in historical time: furthermore, 'what is', politically, never lasts. Thinking as citizens, this means that we must not assume that the present international system is the best of all possible worlds, or that it will last indefinitely.

▶ From Athens to Westphalia

Before recorded history, humans lived in family groups (loosely defined) and tribes, subsisting on gathering and hunting. Life was nomadic. Millennia later, there are still vestiges of these ways of life.

Alongside settled agriculture, beginning about 10,000 BCE, came more static forms of association, including villages and towns. The first identifiable 'civilizations' were in Sumeria and Egypt, beginning in the fourth millennium BCE; others followed in the eastern Mediterranean, and then in India (the Harappa) and China (the Shang). Though nomads persisted, as they still do, political power became more fixed and centralized as a variety of territorial units took shape within developing civilizations, in the form of tribes, city-states, kingdoms and empires. Violence took place between these units, driven by fear, gain and honour; and warrior classes developed.

The emergence of the Greek city-states after the eighth century BCE was of special significance, not least because of their immense legacy of texts about philosophy, arts and science, and especially war and politics (a word derived from *polis*, meaning 'city-state'). For students of IR, one book – *The History of the Peloponnesian War* – by the Greek historian and general Thucydides is of continuing interest. Focused on the long conflict between Athens and Sparta (431–404 BCE), the book is a foundational text of the approach to IR called 'realism' (see Chapter 3), which seeks to account for relations between political units 'as they are', not 'as they ought to be'.

Confronted by the challenges of living under anarchy in the ancient world, empires grew in all continents. The drivers were the struggle for security, territorial ambition and the search for prestige. The great empires included the Shang in the second millennium BCE in China, and Alexander the Great's extension of the empire of the Greeks to Egypt and northern India in the fourth century BCE. In the third century BCE Rome took over part of Alexander's collapsing empire and began its own climb to imperial glory. After dominating large parts of the Mediterranean world and beyond, Rome itself fell in 476 CE to Germanic tribes from the north. But it was nearly a thousand years later before its eastern empire finally collapsed, when Constantinople was captured by the rising imperial power of the Ottomans.

Outside Europe and its borderlands, no empire was as notable as that ruled over by Ashoka, the Buddhist emperor of India. For three decades in the third century BCE, his enlightened leadership led to the renunciation of warfare, support for the education of women, the practice of toleration, and praise for the richness of heterodoxy. Toleration in a multi-religious political entity was a virtue also advanced by Akbar the Great, a Muslim emperor in India in the sixteenth century CE. But, far to the north, an empire of a very different complexion had taken shape at the beginning of the thirteenth century following the unification of Mongol tribes by Genghis Khan. Over the next two hundred years, success at war, not the arts of peace, resulted in the Mongols dominating the world's largest contiguous empire, stretching across the Eurasian landmass.

Life in Europe during the Middle Ages was characterized by a more complex mixture of religious and political authority. Based on feudalism, a system developed in China a thousand years earlier, the Holy Roman Emperor and the Pope stood at the apex. Feudal society was characterized by hierarchical relationships rooted in power rather than on common feelings of identity. At the bottom of society were the serfs, who existed in a condition of slavery, owned by the local lord and required to undertake specific duties in return for minimal protection and rights. For the masses, identity was divided between the local (village level) and the universal ('Christendom'). 'Nations' in the modern sense did not exist. The nobility in different lands had more in common with each other (including language) than with their own subjects. But shared outlooks did not prevent conflict between the nobility, as ambitious families struggled endlessly to achieve or hang on to power.

Central to this picture of struggle is the thesis advanced by sociologist and historian Charles Tilly. In a series of works, he has explained the rise of the modern state in relation to the demands of war. As time passed, he argued, the accumulation and exercise of military power required increasingly specialized and expensive means – guns, gunpowder, and huge armies and navies. As war became a growing burden on the resources of feudal leaders, kings had to develop appropriate administrative institutions, and notably the ability to raise taxes. This was summed up in Tilly's influential thesis about the emergence of the modern state: '*war* made the *state*, and the *state* made *war*'.

The violent struggles between Europe's rulers were often inflamed, and sometimes driven, by religion. The culmination of this was the Thirty Years War (1618–48). The origins of the war included struggles over the balance of power between the Habsburgs and the Bourbons – rulers of the Holy Roman Empire and the kingdom of France respectively – but it was importantly a religious war between Catholics and Protestants. Though it by no means put an end to religious conflicts within states, it was Europe's last major inter-state religious war. Fighting chiefly focused on central Europe where, in the German lands, population losses were estimated at 12 to 13 million people out of a population of approximately 20 million. As a result of such catastrophic destruction, the Thirty Years War became a turning point in the development of the modern state.

The Peace of Westphalia in 1648 consisted of several treaties that are now seen as transformational in the consolidation of certain trends in state formation and that, as such, remain of symbolic importance in the making of the modern states-system. This 'Westphalian system' confirmed not only the outcome of the war on the ground (border changes, for example) but also legitimized the growth of state power and the further breaking up of the supposedly universal church. Key to both developments was the endorsing of state sovereignty (see box) and the principle of *cuius regio, eius religio* ('whose rule, his religion'). It was now for the sovereign to dictate the religion of the state. By legitimizing sovereign equality and the idea of 'what the king or queen says, goes', the Westphalian system accelerated the homogenization of life within modern states, and created the context for future struggles between them.

As it developed, the Westphalian system became synonymous with the maturing of an ideology of 'statism', the convergence of political loyalty as well as decision-making power at the state level. This became complete with the invention and mobilization of the 'imagined community' (Benedict Anderson's phrase) of the modern nation.

Sovereignty

The modern international system has juridical sovereignty as its ordering principle. Sovereignty is defined as the supreme right to exercise exclusive authority (law-making and law-enforcing) over a territory and people. This means that there is equality between sovereign units, which in turn implies anarchy (no power above the sovereign state). It is the entangled and multifaceted relationships between such sovereign entities that give international relations their character, significance and fascination.

▶ The nationalizing of the sovereign state

The international system with which we are familiar today consolidated and spread globally in the three centuries between the end of the Thirty Years War and the break-up of the colonial empires after the Second World War. In detail, there were many twists in the story, as developments took place at different rates in different places.

The Westphalian settlement legitimized sovereignty in relation to a particular image of ruler and ruled. Sovereignty as the 'divine right of kings' was personified by Louis XIV, 'the Sun King' who reigned between 1643 and 1715 and famously (may have) declared 'L'État, c'est moi' (literally: 'The state is me'). This model was decisively challenged by the French Revolution, whose rallying cry in 1789 was 'Liberté,

Égalité, Fraternité' – the famous trinity of *popular* sovereignty. The Revolution took place in the name of 'the people', and the people were equated with 'the nation'. This false but powerful synthesis contributed in nineteenth-century Europe to a major shift taking place from ultimate allegiance to a person to allegiance to the idea of the nation. Political leaders were not slow in developing and mobilizing the national ideal to promote industrialization, capitalism, unity at home between classes and religions, and the maximization of the state's military potential.

Nations and nationalism

The standard definition of a 'nation' focuses on the idea of a population, usually in a distinct territory, that shares a common language, ethnic identity, history, religion and culture. 'Nationalism' is the political expression of this sense of national identity, most prominently in the claim to self-determination.

A state is a territorial political unit: a nation is a people sharing a particular identity, regardless of the political arrangements. Confusingly, many people use the words 'nation' and 'state' interchangeably. This is not the only confusion. True nation-states, in which a very high proportion of the citizenry share the same national identity, are rare. Out of today's 196 sovereign states, there are only about ten proper nation-states, with Japan as the biggest. Most are multinational. The nation-state is therefore largely a fiction, though it has gained currency in international law. International relations, like all politics, are full of fuzzy language.

Nationalism in the nineteenth century occasionally produced great tension between the powers in Europe, and it required the institution of diplomacy to operate at its best to prevent competition getting out of hand. In the decades after 1815, following the defeat of Napoleon, diplomacy rose to the task in the institution of the 'Concert of Europe'. But, as the century progressed, so did the growth of assertive cultures of chauvinism and militarism alongside nationalism. Major war was still largely avoided in Europe itself, but the great powers played out the 'great game' of empires elsewhere.

It was not an accident that the extension of European power throughout the world coincided with the rise of the national idea. As European powers mobilized chauvinistic collective identities and fuelled the engines of the industrial revolution with nationalist vigour, they acquired the decisive war-making potential to conquer and colonize overseas. The colonized, in their turn, learned from their colonizers. In the twentieth century the peoples of Asia, Africa and South America developed and asserted their own national identities, sought independence from their imperial rulers, and demanded their own sovereign states. Together, therefore, a combination of statism, nationalism and imperialism transformed Europe's Westphalian order into today's global international system of sovereign (so-called) nation-states.

In the process just described, the international system swallowed up or incorporated all the political forms that had preceded it. Some of these earlier forms still exist – tribes and nomads, for example – but the nation-state system, underpinned by the idea of sovereignty, became dominant everywhere, and now appears unassailable. Throughout history, this has been the presumption of dominant political forms, now long vanished.

▶ The Great Reckoning

Reading history backwards, this account of the rise and rise of an international system based on sovereign states might appear entirely persuasive. But recall the other possible trajectories mentioned earlier, and remember the great transformations through history. Is there any reason to suppose that radical change has come to an end? Five contemporary challenges to the dominance of the sovereign state as the basic unit of political life globally give pause for thought:

First, as a unit of defence Nuclear weapons and intercontinental missiles put an end to the idea that, if one's armed forces are powerful enough, the national heartland can be defended. Back in the 1950s, IR theorist John Herz argued that the basic defence function of the territorial state had been indefinitely undermined. Until a reliable defence against a missile attack with nuclear weapons can be developed, all states must ultimately remain vulnerable.

Second, as a unit of authority Sovereignty, invariably associated with the rights of governments rather than their responsibilities towards their populations, has seen a shift since the end of the Second World War away from the principle of exclusive authority. The latter has been eroded by the Universal Declaration of Human Rights (1948), the Genocide Convention (1948), the doctrine of humanitarian intervention (especially in the 1990s), the United Nations' (UN) 'human security' agenda (1994), the establishment of the International Criminal Court (1998), and the UN's endorsing of Responsibility to Protect principles (2005). Such developments reflect the growing significance of individuals (and not just states) in international relations and mark a potentially radical change in humankind's common sense about living globally.

Third, as a unit of collective identity The standard image of a state as comprising a relatively homogenous, self-determining and discrete nation is being undermined by migration, devolution, globalization and the spread of global civil society groups committed to world citizenship, environmentalism and peace. In the European Union (EU), sovereignty is 'pooled' and a post-national political culture has been explored. The sociologist Ulrich Beck has speculated about a 'cosmopolitan Realpolitik' in which 'cosmopolitan states' in a globalizing world transcend their national histories in pragmatic co-operative politics.

Fourth, as a unit of economic activity Some observers of the rapid momentum of globalization in the 1990s argued that the state was becoming increasingly irrelevant in face of the dynamics of the global marketplace (see Chapter 6). In 2013 Dan Smith calculated that only 27 states have a gross national income greater than the revenue of Walmart, while 50 states have populations smaller than that company's global workforce. The international system is not 'post-international', as IR theorist James Rosenau suggested in 1990, though the dynamics of globalization continue to throw up questions about power and authority across the world.

Fifth, as units of political independence To be sovereign was once assumed to be synonymous with real independence. Today, the four challenges just described leave political independence as a symbol more than a reality: there is no alternative to interdependence. This is underlined by the remarkable growth of international institutions and global governance, ranging from the UN at the pinnacle (multi-functional and almost universal), to intergovernmental institutions (IGOs) with significant but more limited remits (such as the nuclear non-proliferation regime, or economic bodies like the Association of Southeast Asian Nations), to international non-governmental organizations (INGOs) such as Amnesty International. The *Yearbook of International Organizations* in 2013 recorded over 66,000 different sorts of IGOs and INGOs, with approximately 1,200 being added each year, and most since 1975. As a result of these remarkable changes, international politics increasingly take place within a densifying web of institutional constraints. Even for the most powerful states, dreams of political 'independence' and 'freedom' are like the Cheshire Cat in *Alice in Wonderland*: the smile lingers, but the reality has disappeared.

Will the (Westphalian) international system see off these five challenges? It has without doubt proved adaptive and resilient over the centuries. In 1917 the Bolsheviks inaugurated a world revolution to overthrow it, but within their first decade they were adjusting to the system more than vice versa. Might things be different in future?

Subsequent chapters will show that humankind is facing a concatenation of profound challenges to business as usual: I call it the 'Great Reckoning'. Business as usual (whether the Westphalian system, patriarchy or capitalism) is no longer seen by many to be working in the human interest, or in the interests of the natural world on which we ultimately depend. The international system is dysfunctional in relation to the need for more effective collective action in the face of common global threats such as climate change, nuclear proliferation, food and water insecurity, population growth and so on. But collective agreements are difficult, because in this self-help world competition and mistrust remain the default settings of nation-states.

One rational response to the need for more collective outlooks and decision-making would be to move towards centralizing authority in the form of world government. Such reasoning seems fanciful, if not an actual nightmare to majority opinion globally, at a time when the national idea is asserted with more force than ever in some countries. Moreover, the newly emerging economic powers (the so-called BRICs – Brazil, Russia, India and China) are stubborn champions of the trappings of sovereignty. The familiar international system therefore seems to have much life left in it, short of a global catastrophe.

The big picture of world politics today consists of growing tension between the traditional ordering principle of the territorial sovereign state (for security, prosperity and cultural identity), increasingly insistent global threats (notably climate change) and powerful transnational dynamics (such as globalization and global governance). When we assess the various global changes in relation to the traditional 'texture' of the international, we must try to understand that we are but a dot in a human story of several million years, with the potential (but not guarantee) of millions more years to come. We are bit players in a drama, global human history, whose curtain has barely opened – indeed, whose script is still being argued over.

3

Theories, concepts, debates

'Of all the terms that we employ in treating human affairs, those of natural and unnatural are the least determinate in their meaning.'

Adam Ferguson

The introductory chapters claimed that international relations matter because they impact on all levels of human existence, from geopolitical clashes between superpowers with the capability to destroy the world to the personal biographies of each of us. Not surprisingly, the community of IR scholars who try to make sense of it all has proved to be notoriously argumentative, and this chapter will describe the major fault-lines between them. The stakes could not be higher; no wonder we argue.

▶ Arguing the world

A traditional way of teaching IR to students has involved recalling its 'Great Debates'. Today, this approach is thought unfashionable – too simplifying – but the image of a discipline in permanent dispute with itself remains accurate. This makes life decidedly tough for those searching for quick, simple and agreed answers to the biggest political questions.

Being a student of IR is never easy. For a start, the subject matter is vast. IR is not 'current affairs', 'diplomatic history', 'foreign policy' or 'comparative politics'; it is all these things, and much more: its issues extend throughout the humanities and social sciences. To be a student of IR requires an understanding of history, philosophy, psychology, sociology and economics, as well as politics. Opinions are easy to come by – society is full of know-alls keen to offer one-liners about the state of the world. Informed analysis and judgement, however, require the sharpening of multiple intellectual tools.

IR specialists argue about three broad sets of questions:

1 **Reality:** what are the categorical elements of international relations (the units, the actors, the agenda)?

2 **Knowledge:** how can we best accumulate reliable information and interpretation?

3 **Ethics:** how should we act?

In their disputes over these matters, the community of IR scholars has divided into various schools, each with their own literature, language and leaders. Presently, the most influential schools, in alphabetical order, are classical, structural and other versions of realism, constructivism, critical realism, critical theory (Frankfurt School and neo-Gramscian), the English School, feminism, green theory, historical sociology, liberal theory and its variants, Marxist (and neo-Marxist) theory, neoliberalism, normative theory, peace studies, post-colonialism, post-structuralism and rational choice theory. Non-specialists probably find such a list bewildering, conjuring up images of angels dancing on the head of a pin. This would be a mistake, for the biggest issues of all are at stake.

▶ The fault-lines

The great contestations in IR can be mapped in relation to four major fault-lines:

1 realism versus idealism

2 science versus judgement

3 globalism versus state-centrism

4 critical versus mainstream theory.

What follows is a snapshot of the issues involved.

1 Realism versus idealism

This fault-line was the first of IR's so-called 'Great Debates', though its protagonists in the two decades after 1919 rarely engaged directly with each other. The first idealists were the liberal internationalists who acted as the midwives of the academic project of IR. They envisaged a world of reason, law and morality, and put their hopes in new international organizations; they believed lasting peace is possible. Against them, realist critics argued that such idealists (or 'utopians') engaged the world 'as it ought to be' rather than 'as it is'. The realists focused their attention on states and struggles for power; on the domination of expediency over principle, and hence the inevitability of conflict. They asserted that there are no happy endings in international relations.

The labels 'realist' and 'idealist' leave a lot to be desired. No one, including 'idealists', wants to be thought of as unrealistic, having ideas of no practical relevance. Realists thereby gained an important advantage over other theorists when they appropriated the 'realist' label, though one cannot always be sure what is behind their own label.

Who are the real realists?

William E. Scheuerman, in *The Realist Case for Global Reform* (2011), contrasted the standard image of realists as rejecting morality and the possibility of positive change with a group of thinkers from the mid-twentieth century that he labelled 'Progressive Realists'. Although the members of the group he identified (led by E.H. Carr, John Herz, Hans J. Morgenthau and Reinhold Niebuhr) have traditionally been praised for their brilliance by mainstream realists, their radical and progressive theorizing has been marginalized or entirely overlooked. The overlooked ideas include the spread of 'community' internationally, world government, nuclear disarmament, planetary perspectives on security, and the place of morality in politics. Such views are normally identified with forward-looking 'idealism', not static realism. We should be wary of crude labels and, rather than relying on textbooks, go back to reading the original work of the most original thinkers.

Over the decades, debates *between* realism and idealism have been matched by debates *within* these intellectual tribes. Significant differences have arisen among realists, for example, although 'realism' as a brand remains the dominant approach in IR globally.

The key division within realism followed the publication of Kenneth Waltz's *Theory of International Politics* in 1979. By giving us a better understanding of the importance of structure and its effects, Waltz opened up a gap between 'classical realism' on one side and his own 'structural realism' (or 'neo-realism') on the other. While realists agree on the *character* of international relations (the primacy of sovereign states, the struggle for power, the expectation of conflict and so on), the two branches divide over the fundamental driver of international behaviour. For classical realists, it is human nature; for neo-realists, it is the structure of the international system.

Structure

The idea of structure is central to understanding international relations. A structure is a set of relations that exist independently of an actor. An actor (or agent) is a person or organization (such as a state) able to make things happen. Structures, made up of a complex of ideas, institutions and material power, help explain the actions of actors. Key structures within a society include patriarchy and class. In international relations, the structure of the international system is paramount, and different schools give different weight to the power of structure to shape attitudes and behaviour. For structural realists, anarchy constrains state agents to act according to a logic that maximizes security, whereas idealists argue that there is scope for peace-promoting agency on the part of states and individuals. A sensible compromise recognizes that structures always make a difference, but that powerful agents are sometimes able to bring about change from one structural condition to another, occasionally for the general good.

The intellectual tribe of 'idealism', which has always been divided into more family groupings than that of 'realism', has been marginalized for much of the period since the Second World War as scholars (especially those hoping to have the ear of politicians) have focused on military-strategic questions. But idealist concerns never disappeared. During the Cold War, explicitly value-oriented peace research maintained a toehold, while the persistence of global poverty and the outbreak of bloody wars kept liberal specialists in 'applied ethics' busy, discussing global justice and the relevance of 'just war' thinking. Idealist theorizing has invariably been infused with 'cosmopolitan' values, which in turn means that human rights, applied universally, are considered an essential building block in foreign policy.

Idealist thinking has often been dismissed as 'warm thoughts', but liberal approaches have sometimes shown that they are as comfortable with explicitly social scientific methods as any. In the 1980s, for example, 'neo-liberal institutionalists' explored the multiple relations that take place across borders beyond those conducted through the foreign and defence ministries of governments, and pointed to the potential for international co-operation through institution-building. Central to this approach was the view that the international system offers the possibility of positive pay-offs for all ('absolute gains'), and with it the prospect of stability and peace between states. This verdict is in direct opposition to the neo-realists discussed earlier, who consider the international system to be essentially competitive. For neo-realists, states must focus on their power position: what matters is 'relative gains'.

An influential version of idealism since the 1990s has been 'democratic peace theory' (DPT). This approach, backed by more social scientific (quantitative) research than any other in IR, rests on the assumption that the anarchical international system is open to different behavioural logics: states can shape how the system works, not simply be shaped by it. Accordingly, DPT theorists showed statistically that states with democratic institutions and cultures do not go to war with one other, and that a system of democratic states would therefore be a peaceful one. The DPT remains controversial but it has been politically significant, influencing both the liberal Bill Clinton and the 'neo-con' George W. Bush.

2 Science versus judgement

'Science' has long been an aspiration of some specialists in IR. In the 1950s and 1960s the rise of 'behaviouralism' in the social sciences in the United States sought to transfer the methods of the natural sciences into the study of human behaviour. The new language of positivist social science was introduced, with terms like hypotheses, models, paradigms, systems analysis and game theory. Behaviouralism promised to bring 'objectivity' into the study of Cold War IR.

Positivism

This disputed term, central to the social scientific approach, is generally understood as a commitment to a unified scientific method between the natural and social sciences. Positivism involves the ideal of objectivity, and a belief in the primacy of empirical claims to knowledge. The only robust findings in international relations, therefore, are said to be those that have not been 'falsified'. The DPT is defended by its supporters on these grounds.

Traditional IR specialists, trained in history and philosophy, reacted strongly against behaviouralism and its hopes, promises and pretensions. Traditionalists argued that the study of human society is radically different from that of the natural world: the relationship of observer and observed is quite different, for example, when analysing terrorism as opposed to analysing a lump of rock. 'Objectivity' is seen as an illusion in studying human society: interpretation and judgement are what matter. ('Judgement' – assessing evidence before coming to a conclusion – is necessary in science, of course, but judgement about politics is categorically different, for there can be no claim to objectivity, and world affairs are not a laboratory in which 'experiments' can be conducted.)

Debates between social science and historical-philosophical judgement go on, and sometimes the real world gets overlooked in arguments over method. In the 1960s methodological debate, this did not matter, as both sets of proponents broadly agreed that the real world was essentially one of anarchy and state rivalry in pursuit of the national interest: what separated the proponents was how it should and could be studied.

One powerful social scientific approach, especially in the United States, has been 'rational choice theory'. Cultural and other variables within states are played down in favour of focusing on the rational (strategic) calculations of governments; this entails the weighing of the costs and benefits of a given action, together with an assessment of the likely rational reactions of others. Based on these calculations, it is claimed that governments can then make rational choices about the highest net 'pay-off'. Rational choice theory is criticized by traditionalists on the grounds that it is based on some notion of 'rational man' rather than the complex flesh-and-blood decision-makers always thrown up by history.

3 Globalism versus state-centrism

If the science/judgement fault-line has been about method rather than actually existing international relations, the contestation between globalism and state-centrism is almost wholly about the character of the real world. The term 'globalism' here refers to an image of world politics beyond state-to-state relations in the international system. Instead, a complex transnational network of relationships across borders is foregrounded, involving many sorts of actors interacting at different levels. Two powerful strands of globalism emerged in the 1970s, one liberal-inspired, the other neo-Marxist. Both challenged the then dominant state-centric (realist) image.

At the forefront of the liberal strand of globalism was the publication in 1971 of *Transnational Relations and World Politics* by Robert Keohane and Joseph Nye, followed in 1977 by the same authors' *Power and Interdependence*. Against mainstream state-centrism, Keohane and Nye described a world of 'pluralism' and 'complex interdependence'. States were still seen as important actors, but recognition was demanded for the growing importance of transnational actors such as non-governmental organizations, multinational corporations and even individuals. A shift of attention was also demanded: from state-centrism's focus on foreign and defence policy decision-makers ('soldiers and diplomats') to networks of people and organizations conducting multi-level relations across borders.

In practice, the images of the real world held by transnationalists and realists are less clearly drawn than just described. Realists do not deny that transnational relations take place; they only challenge their significance. Transnationalists for their part do not deny the role played by military security; they only question the convictions of realists about its centrality.

In the 1990s this debate was revisited following the supercharged impact of 'globalization'. As a result of the latter's dynamics leading to the image of a 'shrinking planet' (see Chapter 6), globalization theorists argued that states and nations and their boundaries were becoming of ever-decreasing significance. James Rosenau, mentioned earlier, claimed that world politics had reached a 'post-international' phase.

The most prominent protagonist of the neo-Marxist strand of globalism was Immanuel Wallerstein. His four-volume *The Modern World System*, published between 1974 and 2011, explained the emergence of a one-world system associated with the expansion of capitalism. A related Marxist-inspired approach came from 'Third World' scholars developing 'dependency theory'. Using structural arguments about the overwhelmingly powerful workings of the global capitalist economy, they sought to explain the continuing economic dependence of newly independent former colonies. These ideas had significant influence on non-Western thinking about the emerging economic order in the 1960s and 1970s, but they were marginalized in Western IR. In the 1980s neo-Marxist approaches became more mainstream, with attention being given to the sophisticated ideas of the early communist thinker Antonio Gramsci (1891–1937).

Whereas mainstream IR was primarily concerned with state-centrism, the balance of power and international order, neo-Marxist globalist approaches were primarily concerned with the power of capitalism, and the ways in which profit, poverty and exploitation transcended state boundaries. As a result, socio-economic classes and multinational companies were seen as key actors across the world, and human emancipation (as opposed to state power) was advanced as the guiding operational principle.

4 Critical versus mainstream theory

Although mainstream approaches to IR since the 1940s have been dominated by versions of realism and liberalism, there have always been radical alternatives, such as peace research and neo-Marxist approaches. Since the 1980s a group of 'alternative approaches' has coalesced under the label 'critical theory'. The political economist Robert W. Cox categorized all social theory into 'problem-solving' or 'critical', echoing the 1930s distinction of the famous Frankfurt School between 'traditional' and 'critical' theory. Traditional, or problem-solving, theory takes existing international institutions and norms as a given, and seeks to make them work better, while critical theory attempts to stand outside the situation as it exists and offers critique and vision in the interests of human progress. Insider (problem-solving) theories such as realism and liberalism focus on problems *within* the international status quo, while outsider (critical) approaches focus on the very problem *of* the global status quo.

Challengers to the problem-solving mainstream come in various forms, and some would not consider themselves, strictly speaking, *critical* in the Cox/Frankfurt meaning. Feminist theorists, for example, are agreed about the need to eliminate the 'malestream's' gender bias, but they are divided on much else, embracing a spectrum of standpoints from biological determinism to postmodernism. Feminist IR agrees only that a richer understanding of how the world works is possible after addressing Cynthia Enloe's mind-opening question: 'Where are the women?' Similarly, proponents of 'green theory' differ in political orientation, but share a common view about the need to go beyond problem-solving. In their case, they advocate international relations with a green lens, highlighting the global significance of climate change, for example.

The different intellectual tribes espousing critical theory argue with one another at least as much as with the mainstream, and theory often takes precedence over engagement with the contemporary international agenda. A major fault-line exists between Frankfurt School critical theory and post-structural/post-colonial theory. The former seeks to bring Enlightenment ideas such as emancipation and equality into the theory and practice of international relations, but these values are attacked by poststructuralist/post-colonial theorists for claiming to be 'universalist' while being 'Eurocentric'. Poststructuralist theorists are the most extreme voices challenging the theoretical claims of all other schools of IR, but their view that all knowledge is radically uncertain invites the riposte: why, then, should theirs be believed above all others?

▶ No hiding place

The picture portrayed above is one of permanent argumentation. Whether one considers these apparently unbridgeable fault-lines as undermining the very idea of an academic 'discipline', or whether one celebrates it as 'many flowers blooming', is a matter of personal choice. Before deciding, two points should be considered. First, contestation, claim and counter-claim are ways by which knowledge evolves. And second, the agenda of IR is truly momentous, whether it is dealing with the causes of war or the goal of human emancipation, whether it involves explaining the constraints of anarchy or analysing the dilemmas facing policy-makers. What is at stake can be illustrated with reference to two contentious issues over the past 25 years, one about the real world, the other about how to think about it.

In 1989 political scientist and policy adviser Francis Fukuyama published 'The End of History', an article arguing that the collapse of communism meant the end of ideological cleavages and the emergence of liberal democracy as the final form of government. In 1993 Samuel P. Huntington published a counter-theory entitled 'The Clash of Civilizations', arguing that the basic building blocks of human society have been civilizations, differentiated from each other by tradition, language, culture and especially religion. These civilizational distinctions, he insisted, were historical and would not foreseeably disappear; the cultural differences between the 'major' civilizations would be the great clashes of the future, and particularly between Muslim and non-Muslim civilizations. Moreover, deeper global interaction would not homogenize people, but would make them more conscious of their differences. As a result, according to Huntington, history would return to normal following the global ideological confrontation of the Cold War. Much follows from these different understandings of the real world, depending on whether one thinks the great cleavages of history are behind us, or whether it is indefinitely one of business as usual. One might conclude, of course, that both theories have got it wrong.

One of the biggest recent contestations about method in IR has focused on the rise of 'constructivism', an approach that is not itself an 'IR theory', but which has had a major impact on IR. Unlike realism, constructivism does not provide a categorical picture of the real world (states and their strategies) but is instead a social theory seeking to explain how human society works. It focuses on reality not as a static phenomenon but as something made and remade through 'intersubjective' human understandings. Reality, in short, is a human construction. From this perspective, the 'anarchy' characterizing the international system is a construction of ideas and related institutions, not a reality of nature like a mountain. As constructivist theorist Alexander Wendt famously observed, 'Anarchy is what states make of it.'

If one follows this argument, ideas are central to *constituting* international behaviour, and not simply to trying to *explain* it, as in the traditional image of the role of theory. In other words, theory has a role in inventing or replicating or reordering global realities. In this sense, Fukuyama and Huntington were providing much more than academic explanations of the state of the world; consciously or not, they were providing policy-guiding principles to shape the thinking of state leaders and others. There is always much at stake in IR; this is why the intellectual tribal feuding will go on.

The academic discipline of IR will continue to agonize over matters that demand complex answers; snappy verdicts on the issue of the day are not our business, only a temptation. To be a student of IR, at any age, is to be challenged to make sense of disputed interpretations of history, the confusions of the present, and the ideas of several disciplines – all in relation to the biggest political questions of all. IR leaves its students with no hiding place.

Fear, power, security

*'Few people can be happy unless
they hate some other person,
nation or creed.'*

Bertrand Russell (attributed)

Arguing the world is often about fear and power. These drivers of human behaviour are sometimes in the background, but commonly are at centre stage. This is evident from such ancient nostrums as *Homo homini lupus est* ('Man is a wolf to man') and *animus dominandi* (the 'will to power'). According to such ideas, we are trapped by 'human nature' and the 'human condition' in a cage of selfishness and aggression, uncertainty and danger. Nowhere has this been argued more strongly than when nations and states interact in the arena of international relations.

▶ The 'state of nature'

Fear is a primordial emotion, with both rational and irrational dimensions. On the one hand, fear has been of decisive evolutionary benefit to the human species. Without it, humans would not have shown the prudence that led our ancestors into learning how to preserve food for their families during winter or devising defences against dangerous beasts. Without fear, the human animal would not have flourished.

In other contexts, fear can have highly negative consequences. In politics, fear can promote misperceptions and overreactions; and unscrupulous leaders can manufacture fear to manipulate populations to their will. And when fear takes hold, whether it is real or manufactured, international politics can become the site for some of the worst excesses of 'Man's inhumanity to Man'. In this regard, it is important to remember that nine states today, including the biggest, are so driven by fear (among other factors) that they base their defence policies, ultimately, upon a declared willingness in some circumstances to kill tens of millions of people, indiscriminately, with nuclear weapons.

Fatalistic readings of international relations, arguing that conflict is natural and should be prepared for, has been common since the earliest times: in ancient China in the writing of Sun Tzu about 'The Necessity of War', and in Plato's view in ancient Greece that humans are not naturally inclined to live peacefully together. In the twentieth century the Nazi philosopher Carl Schmitt asserted that all 'truly political relations' are of the 'friend–enemy' type. At the root of much of this thinking is a conviction in the inescapable aggressiveness, selfishness and competitiveness of something identified as 'human nature'. For countless commentators through the centuries, human nature has been considered the starting and finishing point for all things political, social and economic: it drives behaviour and constrains what can be achieved.

There is a counter-view. This argues that human nature and the 'human condition' are not inescapable realities: they are realities only in the sense that they are ideas that human societies have internalized, and so can be changed. In the words of the international lawyer and philosopher Philip Allott, human nature and the human condition are 'powerful self-fulfilling myths' that have gripped human imaginations and deformed human potential. As long as we continue to internalize such beliefs, Allott is convinced, international relations will remain characterized by 'war and the infantile rivalries of states, systematic injustice and the countless forms of corrupt and corrupting power'. This view, idealist in the sense that ideas are basic to global realities, informs this book. More common among IR specialists, however, has been a fatalistic image of international politics trapped in 'the state of nature'.

Hobbes and the state of nature

The 'state of nature' was a common thought experiment among political theorists in the seventeenth and eighteenth centuries. It supposed a time before humans were organized into civil society, and this absence of governmental authority has sometimes been seen as analogous to anarchy in international relations – a *state* of war if not a *condition* of actual fighting. Under such conditions, as explained earlier, 'self-help' has been considered a necessity: there is nobody else on whom to rely in the struggle for power and security.

The standard reference is *Leviathan* (1651), written by Thomas Hobbes at the time of the English Civil War. In a key passage he said:

'Hereby it is manifest that, during the time men live without a common power to keep them all in awe, they are in that condition which is called war, and such a war as is of every man against every man. For WAR consisteth not in battle only, or the act of fighting, but in a tract of time wherein the will to contend by battle is sufficiently known; and therefore the notion of time is to be considered in the nature of war as it is in the nature of foul weather. For as the nature of foul weather lies not in a shower or two of rain but in an inclination thereto of many days together, so the nature of war consisteth not in actual fighting but in the known disposition thereto during all the time there is no assurance to the contrary.'

Life in the state of nature is 'nasty, brutish and short' in Hobbes's famous phrase. In the late 1940s John Herz called this a condition of 'kill or perish', which in turn he labelled 'the security dilemma'. This fundamental dilemma results from the convergence of the imperative of self-help and the innate capacity of humans to harm one another. What is more, the weapons humans deploy against each other have an inherent ambiguity: what a person or nation can use defensively, for self-protection, can also be used coercively, to try and gain advantage. A shield, to parry blows, is ostensibly 'defensive', but used in conjunction with a sword can be part of an aggressive attack.

The security dilemma is ultimately fuelled by the inability of people to get into the heads of others (the so-called 'other minds problem'). Governments can never fully know the motives and intentions of those who possess weapons that have the capacity to inflict harm upon them. The uncertainty goes further. Prudent governments must not only make judgements about the present motives and intentions of governments with the capacity to do them harm, but they must also try to predict their long-term motives and intentions, and even those of their successors. The security dilemma casts a very long shadow into the future.

With mistrust being the default position of governments in a condition of anarchy and self-help, the only thing they can be certain about is the determination of others to seek to survive and attempt to gain advantage. In such circumstances, co-operation is conditional. It is sometimes fragile. Even supposed 'friends' may be tempted to spy on one other.

Security dilemmas remain plentiful. Can Russian policy-makers today be certain that US interest in ballistic missile defence is simply for national defence, or might it be part of a strategy to build an unassailable coercive capability? Does the development of a 'blue water' Chinese navy represent the modernizing of its warships for enhanced defence, or does it signal a more aggressive role in the South China Sea and beyond? Can Iran's neighbours be confident that its nuclear enrichment programme over the years has simply been for domestic energy security? Are the nuclear tests and military posturing of the regime in North Korea a deterrent strategy on the part of an isolated international pariah, or are they part of a long-term coercive strategy to bring the whole peninsula under its control?

The shadow of the security dilemma is so enveloping that it is not necessary for a government to have a specific enemy for the other minds problem to do its work. In recent decades, for example, the UK homeland has enjoyed an unprecedented sense of security from attack by an enemy state. Even so, Tony Blair's New Labour government in 2005–6 justified its commitment to maintain its strategic nuclear weapons capability for another generation because of the 'certainty of uncertainty' over the very long term. UK strategic planners were as confident as they could be that there would not be a nuclear threat or military assault on the UK over the next ten years, but could they be sure this would remain the case for the following fifty? As Kurt Vonnegut would have commented: 'And so it goes.'

Fear is at the root of the security dilemma and can cause a spiralling of mistrust and mutual arming, but the accumulation of weaponry can have other drivers, from the profits of the 'military–industrial complex' to leaders engaged in masculinist arm-wrestling. Ambition has always been a key factor behind a state's militarization, to increase bargaining power for coercion, and sometimes to engage in war. When a state's aggressive ambitions become obvious, security dilemmas about motives and intentions disappear and are replaced by the certainties of realpolitik. This is what happened on the part of the Western democracies in the late 1930s, when any residual doubts about the ambitions of Nazi Germany were swept aside by Hitler's military moves against Austria and Czechoslovakia. Whether one's motive is defensive or offensive, and whatever one's predicament, power is paramount.

▶ 'Hard' and 'soft' power

Power in international relations is what allows actors (usually, but not always, governments) to achieve their goals. It comes in multiple forms (carrots and sticks); it is contextual (what works in one situation may not work in another); and, if successful, it makes other governments do what they might not otherwise have wanted to do. Not surprisingly, IR is sometimes called the study of 'power politics', though *politics* is hardly conceivable without power, so in this sense the word 'power' is redundant. Power is necessary not only for survival in a world of uncertainty, but also for the achievement of ambitions beyond survival. The iconic IR story of power is the 'Melian Dialogue'.

The Melian Dialogue

The Melian Dialogue is a drama described by Thucydides in his *History of the Peloponnesian War*. In 416 BCE, in the long conflict between Athens and Sparta, the Athenians issued an ultimatum to the people of Melos, a small island whose people had kinship and political ties with Sparta. The Athenian envoys demanded surrender and the payment of tribute on threat of destruction. The Melians claimed the right of neutrality and appealed to the much more powerful Athenians on the grounds of mercy and justice, as well as more pragmatic considerations. Arguments followed that echo down the centuries when political rivals of different power potential confront each other in extreme situations. The brutal and endlessly repeatable words Thucydides put into the mouth of an Athenian envoy were as follows: 'The strong do what they can and the weak suffer what they must.'

Despite the power differentials, the Melians refused to surrender. The Athenians carried out their threat, executed the men they captured, and enslaved the women and children. Melos became an Athenian colony. In time, the Athenian empire itself collapsed, and Melos was restored to what remained of its people.

This drama, together with its aftermath, offers two lessons: the short-term message appears to be 'might is right'; the longer-term message suggests that 'who lives by the sword dies by the sword'. In both cases, power is key.

Fear, power, security

▲ Total war: Berlin 1945.

▲ Separatist war today: Grozny 1999.

REX/A.A. SIPA

▲ Civil war today: Homs 2014.

According to sociologist Daniel Bell, the political world-view of the victorious Bolsheviks in the 1917 Russian Revolution could be reduced to the phrase *kto-kovo* (literally 'who-whom'). In other words, all political relations are between 'dominators and dominated, between users and used'. Politics at the international level are often interpreted this way, with the power to dominate being measured according to material calculations: who has the greater population size, numbers in their armed forces, industrial strength and so on, and who the lesser? But history shows that such crude metrics of power do not easily translate into political or even military success. In 1935 the Soviet dictator Joseph Stalin infamously dismissed the political power of the papacy on the basis of its lack of armed force ('How many divisions does the Pope of Rome have?' he is supposed to have asked). A half-century later, religion and nationalism had come together in central and eastern Europe and trumped Soviet-style communism, even though the latter was backed by overwhelming military capabilities.

A decade earlier, the other superpower, the United States, had learned a similar lesson in actual war. Military history will always highlight the failure of the US, with the overwhelming technological superiority of its forces between 1965 and 1975, to impose its will on Vietnam. Power cannot be reduced to metrics: it is relational and contextual, best understood in terms of the relations of specific actors in specific settings over particular issues.

In the employment of power, an influential distinction has been made by Joseph S. Nye, political scientist and occasional US government insider, between 'hard' and 'soft' power. According to Nye, hard power is exercised through both carrots (varieties of inducements) and sticks (varieties of coercion). Soft power, in contrast, concerns attraction and persuasion. This means getting one's way through agenda-setting or prestige, which may result from cultural or ideological standing, or political success. Nye insists that it does not follow that soft power is necessarily 'good' and hard power necessarily 'bad': these are ethical judgements, he argues, and what matters is not the type of power, but the purpose for which it is exercised. Compare, for example, the use of soft power by al-Qaeda to indoctrinate potential jihadists, and the UN's endorsing of hard power to uphold international law in 1990–91 in the face of Iraq's invasion of Kuwait.

The distinction between hard and soft power echoes an older one between 'power' and 'influence', with influence including notions such as respect, authority and legitimacy. When it comes to achieving one's goals through influence rather than hard power, the trick is for a state to get its way by constructing what Italian Marxist Antonio Gramsci called 'common sense' and French sociologist Michel Foucault later described as 'regimes of truth'. If a state (or any political actor) can make its ideas and authority appear natural or normal ('common sense'), it is well on the way to achieving its goals. The concept of 'hegemon' (see Chapter 8) is relevant here. While theorists in the traditions of Gramsci and Foucault emphasize the power of ideas in embedding authority, realists argue that what matters is military and economic power. In either case, a successful hegemon will not need to use brute force to get its way. On the contrary: the need to employ actual force represents a breakdown of hegemonial authority.

In deciding what will work best in particular circumstances, policy-makers are faced with the difficulty of trying to understand the changing modalities of power and their applicability in different situations. The instruments that generate power change, though perhaps not as quickly as some imagine. Military power, even if in the background, is rarely completely irrelevant. In 2013, after the Obama administration had put on hold the decision to intervene militarily against the

Syrian regime, the ultimate threat of force still played a disciplining role in the Syrian regime's thinking about its commitment to destroy its chemical weapons. One of the important skills of statecraft (see Chapter 5) is to know which type of power – hard or soft – works when, how, where, and in what combination.

▶ The search for security

Regardless of the modalities of power, and whether a state is recognized as one of the powerful or one of the weak, security is a primary goal. A degree of security – being and feeling safe from dangerous threats to one's body and way of life generally – is a need of human social existence. Without relative security – 'absolute' security is an impossibility – persons and collectivities cannot attend to babies and their development, construct communities, or build sustainable and humane states. Security must be a central preoccupation in the practices and theories of international relations.

Being insecure to any significant degree means living a determined life. Chronically insecure states do not excel in economic development, cultural richness or decent levels of human happiness. High levels of insecurity for people can emanate from various sources, with the threat of war being the most urgent. But insecurity can also result from internal weakness (ethnic conflict), bad leaders (whose ambitions outmatch their capabilities) or extreme ideologies (which produce tyranny at home and tension outside).

At the level of individuals, being insecure means being trapped by personal, group or geopolitical dynamics. Poverty, for example, is always powerfully determining. If daily life is entirely dominated by the search for the basic means to survive – food and water – people are deprived of the opportunity to develop more fully as human beings. Human life then becomes little different from that of other animals. In order to explore what it might be to become more fully human, people need both the physical and mental resources to act, and the community and political institutions to give them voice.

Security policy at all levels is deeply political and deeply politicized. Politics is central to engaging with the three basic dimensions of security: the referent-object (who or what is to be secured), the threats to that referent (what the priority dangers are), and the policies to be chosen for meeting the threats identified. Security is the more deeply politicized because the very word raises expectations: of resources being mobilized and action being followed through when decisions are taken in its name.

One's ideas about each of the three dimensions of security derive from underlying political outlooks, socialization and position. For example, radical jihadists prioritize the referent-object of the wider religious community beyond the boundaries of mere states; nuclear disarmers emphasize the threat of a nuclear catastrophe in their calculus of threats; and developing nations in particular, when considering the inevitable question 'How much is enough?' must decide between what to spend on 'human security' as against 'state security'.

Critics sometimes assert that the IR community spends too much time on security issues. What they really mean is that too much attention is paid to security conceived narrowly in terms of traditional military security – especially the 'balance of power' – rather than broader conceptions of security involving human rights, economic justice and threats from 'climate chaos' (as the World Wildlife Fund rightly calls it). These are all issues affecting somebody's security, and one of the features of IR debates in recent decades has been the broadening of the agenda from the sovereign priorities of states to viewing international relations as if people really matter (see Chapter 7).

Balance of power

This concept, central to realist thinking, has multiple meanings and is surrounded by controversy about its practical implications. It generally refers to an equilibrium of power whereby the capabilities of one state or combination of states are balanced and checked by the capabilities of others. Some argue that achieving such an equilibrium is difficult, and can be attained only by careful diplomacy. Others, notably structural realists, argue that the international system has an inherent tendency towards equilibrium. Hobbes, whose influential 'state of war' image was outlined earlier, believed that actually existing international relations could and often were ameliorated by policies of prudence and expediency that created an equilibrium of power.

The mainstream understanding of security in IR focuses on the constraints and dynamics imposed by the anarchy imperative; this requires much attention being paid to the monitoring of the balance of power measured primarily in military terms. An alternative approach develops the idea of security in relation to emancipation, in which the possibilities for human flourishing open up as a result of growing freedom from material want, from ignorance, from the deceits of the powerful, and from political and economic tyranny. Contemplating security as emancipation (involving the promotion of human security, human rights, conflict resolution and so on) shows how far the discipline has come in rethinking the international since 1919: the continuing commitment of the UN Security Council Permanent Members and others to rest their 'ultimate' security on genocidal nuclear threats shows how far human society globally still has to go.

5

Conflict, co-operation, statecraft

'Thus it is well to seem merciful, faithful, humane, sincere, religious, and also to be so; but ... it must be understood that a prince, and especially a new prince, cannot observe all those things which are considered good in men, being often obliged, in order to maintain the state, to act against faith, against charity, against humanity, and against religion.'

Niccolò Machiavelli

Probably the most famous witticism about international relations remains the definition of a 'diplomat' offered by an English gentleman, Henry Wotton, in 1604: 'A diplomat is an honest man sent to lie abroad for his country.' The key phrase is often rendered as 'sent abroad to lie' (which is blunt) but the more piquant version ('to lie abroad') embraces the idea both of Machiavellian dissembling and, in the original Elizabethan vernacular, the activity of sleeping around. International relations, in other words, is an arena where what matters is what works. In the abstract, there is a lengthy menu of policy choices of what *might* work; in making the choice, and in its implementation, the skills of statecraft are at a premium. History records that governments have often been found wanting.

▶ The 'posture of gladiators'

Thomas Hardy, over a century ago, wrote: 'War makes rattling good history.' Warfare, for sure, has been central to the history of all peoples and remains a terrible fascination. While not as dominating a concern for many IR scholars as in the past, war must not be ignored: its costs, consequences and ethical dimensions are too enormous. The spiralling crisis in and around the Ukraine during the winter of 2013–14 underlined that the international system remains a 'war system': Russian boots on the ground changed the status of the Crimea; the NATO alliance discussed scenarios; Russian troops mobilized on its border with eastern Ukraine, establishing the context in which pro-Russian activists and opinion across the border could agitate and hope; and the new government in Kiev geared up to defend its territory from internal and external challengers. Little seemed to have changed since Thomas Hobbes had observed that rational governments must adopt the 'posture of gladiators'.

If this persisting image of international relations as a 'state of war', if not always of actual battle, remains valid, two fundamental questions arise: How can we best explain the historic persistence of the dreadful institution of war? And what is war's future? As ever, IR specialists disagree.

On the recurrence of war, there is still no better starting point than Kenneth N. Waltz's classic *Man, the State and War* (1959). Noting the 'bewildering ... variety' of explanations for major war, Waltz categorized them according to arguments about their primary driver: 'within man, within the structure of the separate states, [and] within the state system'. He described these three 'images', or levels, of explanation as follows: 'first-image' theories explain war as a manifestation of an aggressive and ambitious human nature; 'second-image' theories explain war as the result of the aggressive character of some types of states; and 'third-image' theories explain war in relation to the anarchical structure of the international system. Waltz cleverly countered first-image theories by arguing that human nature is one of those ideas that explains everything and therefore nothing: if human nature can be used to explain war, it can equally be used to explain peace. He countered second-image explanations by arguing that war has been engaged in by all types of states at different times, including between states with similar ideologies. His conclusion, based on 'third-image' ideas, was that the most persuasive theory about the causes of war focuses on the structure of anarchy ('war occurs because there is nothing to prevent it').

Most theories of war, regardless of their primary causal explanation, have generally understood the rationale for particular wars to be political. This perspective is above all associated with Karl von Clausewitz and his classic work, *Vom Kriege* (*On War*, published in 1832). Still widely regarded as the greatest philosopher of war, Clausewitz explained that, although war is the realm of violence and chance, with all that these imply for unpredictability, it is essentially a rational instrument of state policy. Thus his famous dictum: 'War is a continuation of politics with an admixture of other means, namely violence.'

As a political instrument, there has been a growing body of opinion since the 1960s arguing that the utility of war is in decline, especially among the most powerful states. This view is based essentially on cost–benefit analysis. The costs of going to war are seen to have been rising (evident in domestic attitudes to the loss of lives and treasure, and the growing lethality of weapons), while the benefits are seen to be decreasing (attempting to control 'foreign' territory these days is ever-more difficult, and of dubious long-term advantage). Based upon such cost–benefit calculations, the verdict of political scientist John Mueller in the late 1980s that major war had become 'obsolescent' looks accurate. But we must be on guard about being too complacent or West-centric about this. Globally, high levels of militarization continue: *The War Report 2012* listed 38 armed conflicts in 24 states and territories with a further 52 states being involved in these conflicts in some way. In excess of 100,000 casualties were recorded (admitted to be 'an extremely conservative' figure) and 28.8 million people were internally displaced because of violence and human rights violations.

As these figures make clear, conflict remains widespread. Since the end of the Cold War there have been numerous civil wars, military interventions and regional conflicts. Some wars have involved appalling levels of casualties, notably the 'Great War of Africa' (in the Congo, 1998–2003) with an estimated 5 to 6 million deaths and massive population displacements. This war, shockingly, was ignored by most of the world. Elsewhere, the 'posture of gladiators' remains at high levels of readiness: in the Middle East (the Arab–Israeli conflict, the Israel–Iran confrontation, the Syrian imbroglio); in South Asia (India–Pakistan); in eastern Europe (Russia–Ukraine); and in East Asia (flashpoints across the Taiwan Straits, in the South China Sea and on the Korean Peninsula). Against all this actual or potential violence – not least the continuing nuclear dangers – Steven Pinker's beguiling image of the rise of 'the better angels of our nature' against violence in his 2011 book of that name looks premature, if not complacent.

The 'harmony of interests'

Liberal ideas about international relations were influential in the early development of academic thinking about IR, especially in the United States and Great Britain. A major theme, dating from the nineteenth century, has been that of the 'harmony of interests' between nations – the international relations equivalent of Adam Smith's 'invisible hand' in economics. According to the harmony of interests aspiration, people act according to a rational calculation of their interests and so work together across borders. Free trade is the mechanism, and their individual rational interests merge into a common interest. The outcome is peace and absolute gain for all.

Liberal optimism was famously evident in Norman Angell's popular book *The Great Illusion: A Study of the Relation of Military Power to National Advantage*, first published in 1909. He argued that war would be futile – it would not pay – but not impossible. The Great War that erupted a few years later tragically endorsed his argument that war indeed does not pay: it also demonstrated that this does not stop war from breaking out and spreading, sometimes to everybody's great surprise.

Our 'better angels' have a long journey, and the political road map is yet to be agreed. In addition to the active and threatened violence just mentioned, new weaponry is being developed, such as drones, that open up novel possibilities for strategies of conflict. So, while the evidence for the decline of war between major powers since the mid-twentieth century looks impressive, it may well be that any 'retreat' from war is the result of the fear of retaliatory violence rather than the spread of virtue: war is worse, not people better. A further check on the Pinker thesis is to remember the propensity of international relations to throw up surprises. We must guard against wishful thinking and contentious (albeit comforting) statistics. A century ago the dangerous illusion among the major powers was the utility of war; today the dangerous illusion may be the robustness and prevalence of peace.

▶ 'Stable peace'

Violent conflict, sustained by the belief that force and the threat of force can indeed sometimes pay, is not about to disappear from international relations in the near future: many believe it will never do so. The dream of pacifist states – disarmed and eschewing violence as an instrument of policy – remains a distant (though necessary) vision. But politics is a pragmatic business, as well as one for visions, and in this regard Voltaire's old adage is a good guide: 'Le mieux est l'ennemi du bien' ('The best is the enemy of the good'). In the foreseeable future, the good consists of politics of co-operation leading towards a condition in which war does not enter into the calculations of ever wider groupings of states, even if disputes arise between them. Such a condition was called 'stable peace' by Kenneth Boulding in the late 1970s. Under it, armed forces are reduced and play an ever more symbolic role; and the commitment to settle issues without violence deepens through economic and social interdependence, common institutions and a shared peace-embracing identity.

The most elaborated academic thinking along these lines is 'security community' theory, originally developed by the IR theorist Karl Deutsch and his associates in the 1950s. The chief model for this theory, as it has developed over the decades, has been the transformation of Europe from total war in the first half of the 1940s to today's institutionalized integration. Integration is the voluntary institutionalization of relations between several states. It is characterized by supranational rather than international decision-making, by economic integration such as the setting up of a common market, and by the building of a political community based on pluralistic politics. European integration, at present focused on the European Union (EU), is undergoing considerable strain in the aftermath of the financial shocks of 2007–8 and the rise of europhobic nationalism. Even so, war between members of the EU remains (almost) unthinkable. This is a remarkable change in what was a cockpit of war historically.

Short of integration, states can co-operate at lower levels, and with different degrees of intensity. Co-operation between states is not always easy, but there is more of it going on every day of the week than some of the images of posturing gladiators discussed earlier might suggest. International law, for example, helps regulate co-operation in different spheres and provides a framework for the settling of disputes. Like plumbing, we become fully aware of the daily workings of international law only when something goes wrong.

At the geopolitical level, a significant practice of co-operation is that involved in attempts to build order through the construction of an 'international society'. Moving beyond the stark image of egocentric states interacting in a 'system', this approach opens the image of governments constructing a 'society' with shared ideas about international order, law and justice, and common outlooks on the balance of power and the responsibilities of major powers. The Concert of Europe after 1815 is invariably put forward as the role model for such a society. The lapse of time since the Concert's demise underlines the fragility of attempts by the major powers to create and sustain an effective international society.

The Concert included states with different domestic political characteristics, showing that international co-operation does not demand close ideological or cultural affinities. The classic expression of the primacy of interests over ideology was given by Viscount Lord Palmerston, UK Foreign Secretary and twice Prime Minister during Queen Victoria's reign. In justifying not going to war against Russia in 1848, he told the House of Commons: 'We have no eternal allies, and we have no perpetual enemies. Our interests are eternal and perpetual, and those interests it is our duty to follow.'

Sustained co-operation depends on shared interests, and if these interests disappear, so does the immediate cause of working together. Shared security interests in particular, and notably alliances against a common enemy, can make the strangest bedfellows. This was exemplified in 1941 by Winston Churchill, the UK Prime

Minister, following Hitler's invasion of the Soviet Union. Now looking forward to the prospect having the Red Army under Stalin fight alongside the UK in a common cause, Churchill – who in 1917 had hoped 'to strangle at birth the Bolshevik State' – announced: 'If Hitler invaded Hell I would make at least a favourable reference to the Devil in the House of Commons.'

The range of areas across which international co-operation is possible is wide – economic, political, cultural and military concerns – and so is the degree of intensity. States may have the most minimal co-operation if they are geographically distant and have few common interactions other than occasionally voting a particular way at the UN. But more robust practices of co-operation can develop into so-called international regimes. These occur when states (and non-state actors) seek to co-operate closely to mitigate or overcome particular problems, and co-ordinate their interests in relation to shared norms and procedures. Arguably the most significant such institution has been the nuclear non-proliferation regime that developed after 1968. Its membership is almost universal, and it has played a role in inhibiting the spread of nuclear weapons. Its contribution to its goal of nuclear disarmament has been less impressive, however, and its future is threatened by the continuing hypocrisy of the nuclear powers in hanging on to their weapons, and the danger that several states might defect from the regime and follow them by developing their own nuclear capabilities.

The possible erosion of the non-proliferation regime gives credence to those who believe that history shows that all international co-operative ventures will eventually collapse. In time, it is often argued, common interest will be undermined by unilateral ambitions. Nonetheless, the liberal hope of interests converging remains strong. The collapse of Soviet communism and its co-option into the global capitalist system gave an enormous boost to this view (see Chapter 6).

The historical record does indeed warn against naive optimism regarding the flowering of international co-operation. Just as ideological enemies can sometimes co-operate when common interests drive them, ideological bedfellows can also disagree radically. This was evident in the bad-tempered exchanges between the Bush administration and the French government over the invasion of Iraq in 2003. States are not people, and so terms like 'friend', from interpersonal relations, are best avoided. Friends do not spy on one other; governments can be expected to, if they think they can get away with it.

If international co-operation works well, public and media interest in international relations tends to wane. It is appropriate therefore to end this section by completing Hardy's words quoted at the start of the chapter. After telling us that war makes 'rattling good history', he added: 'Peace is poor reading.' More's the pity – and the fixation with things warlike, gender specialists argue, is one outcome of the unhealthy masculinization of human culture.

▶ Diplomacy: 'a continuation of war by other means'?

The distinction between 'domestic' politics (supposedly the realm of order) and 'foreign' affairs (supposedly the realm of anarchy) can easily be overdrawn. Domestic politics can be anarchical (in 'failed states' such as Somalia in recent years) or utterly broken (the civil war in Syria since 2011). In contrast, the condition of anarchy in international relations can be compatible with order (South America), and even with predictable peace (the Nordic countries). Nonetheless, the domestic/foreign distinction is sufficient for governments to maintain separate trained specialists, institutions of state and policy processes. Foreign ministries and diplomats responsible for shaping and implementing their country's foreign policy remain important, even if they do not have the same independence they enjoyed in earlier centuries, when slow communications meant that they were less at the beck-and-call of their home governments.

Foreign policy consists of the general attitudes, specific aims and forms of implementation by which governments seek to promote 'the national interest'. The latter is a notoriously slippery concept, though it is one politicians enthusiastically embrace. At one level, the national interest is simply a truism, referring to a state's interest in maximizing security, maximizing prosperity and defending and/or promoting its way of life or ideology. At another level, 'the national interest' is what powerful political groups say it is, and as such is a political appraisal – potentially a cover largely for special pleading. During the apartheid years, South Africa's white government defined the national interest in relation to what was good for its own racial group. Today, UKIP supporters in Great Britain define the national interest in relation to their own anti-European outlook, centred on the UK leaving the EU. Such factional takes on the national interest were immortalized by Charles Wilson, CEO of General Motors, when he declared in 1953: 'What's good for General Motors is good for America.'

Special pleading is but one of the aspects involved in analysing the processes and pathologies of foreign policy-making. The rich literature on this includes: Graham Allison's *The Essence of Decision* (1971), explaining the Cuban Missile Crisis according to three different models of decision-making (decisions as the product of rational actors, organizational processes and bureaucratic politics); Irving Janis's *Groupthink* (1972) on the social dynamics of decision-making, showing how supposedly moral people can make stupid decisions – as relevant for Iraq in 2003 as when it was published; and Robert Jervis's *Perception and Misperception* (1976) on the multiple psychological dimensions of statecraft.

The conduct of foreign policy is invariably difficult, involving as it does interaction with 'other minds' that are largely inaccessible, and other interests likely to be in competition. There is no better contemporary illustration of the difficulty of moving forward in this challenging environment than the contrast between candidate Barack Obama's 'Yes We Can' optimism, and his subsequent experience as President, when he discovered the constraints even on the world's most powerful political figure. He discovered them on a range of issues, from reducing nuclear weapons to closing down Camp Delta at Guantánamo Bay. Complexity is everywhere, and whether one is implementing policy or giving advice, multiple factors must be considered. These include weighing domestic public opinion and commercial interests, assessing the proclivities of liberal democracies and military juntas, and balancing interests in relation to major or minor trading partners. And there are always idiosyncratic matters to consider, especially the personalities of the leaders with whom one is dealing.

REX/Sipa Press

▲ An Obama–Putin summit, but nation does not seem keen to speak to nation. In September 2013 Putin described the relationship as follows: 'We hear each other and understand the arguments. But we simply don't agree. I don't agree with his arguments and he doesn't agree with mine.'

In the light of all this complexity, predicting how others will behave remains a daunting task, and there is no evidence that the foreign ministries of the world (or anybody else) are getting better at it. One need only recall the general level of surprise at the 'Arab Spring' in 2010, or how quickly peaceful protest in Ukraine escalated to the brink of war with Russia in 2014. Twenty-five years earlier, the end of the Cold War – up to that point a seemingly permanent feature of international affairs – came to an end at a speed and in a manner (basically the surrender and dismantling of the Soviet Union) that took the policy world by complete surprise.

The capacity of international relations to shock is endless, despite the huge accumulation of knowledge and increasingly sophisticated information technology. If one takes a decade-long perspective on foreign policy, surprise can be regarded as the norm. Think of Italy's move from being a member of the Axis with Nazi Germany in 1939 to becoming a member of NATO in 1949, or Germany's transformation from the defeated and hated enemy of 1945 to being at the heart of integrating Western Europe in 1955. Such examples should be recalled whenever one is tempted to say that something can *never* happen in international politics.

The difficulty of prediction is one reason some social scientists have been attracted to 'rational choice approaches' to interpreting foreign policy (see Chapter 3). The problem, to recap, is that the approach sounds better in theory than it works in practice. In the actual world of policy-making, 'rational diplomatic man' is a real human being in a particular cultural and political context, facing dilemmas with limited time and information. Real people, in diplomacy as in life in general, cannot be relied upon to act rationally, and certainly not with the same rationality as might be understood by a foreign observer. It remains a continuing task of (and rationale for) diplomats to try to interpret the motives and intentions of these real people acting on behalf of other real governments.

Diplomacy

Protected by rules developed over the centuries (special immunities and privileges), diplomats represent their state, negotiate on its behalf, gather information, and contribute to policy formulation. As such, diplomacy is one of the institutions of the international system, though occasionally (especially in the twentieth century) revolutionary regimes such as the Soviet Union after 1917 and Iran after 1979 have rejected its trappings. Eventually, those regimes adjusted to the institution of diplomacy more than it did to them; but they would have agreed with the stark definition of 'diplomacy' given by the Chinese communist statesman Chou En Lai used as the title of this section, equating diplomacy with war.

A country's diplomatic service has traditionally been at the heart of foreign policy-making and implementation. Depending on the aim of policy, diplomats will advise on using hard or soft power. Their own professional expertise is in negotiation, whether it relates to offering carrots (economic inducements, cultural exchanges, aid, alliance partnership, etc.) or sticks (sanctions, military coercion, withdrawal of diplomats, etc.). In both cases, diplomats will consult with other specialists in government, including the intelligence services. Intelligence gathering (involving the skills of espionage and analysis) is obviously a matter of particular political sensitivity, while the contemplation of the use of military instruments requires the skills of strategists and is of particular significance given the potential costs – in blood, treasure, prestige and power – of getting it wrong.

Diplomacy has had to adjust to many changes. In particular, the independence and influence of diplomatic missions overseas and of foreign ministries at home have declined as a result of the increasing role demanded by most political leaders in foreign affairs, the rise of 'low' politics in the diplomatic agenda (see Chapter 6), and the manner in which communications technology has reduced the distance between governments and their foreign embassies. Some argue, because of this, that diplomats and indeed foreign ministries are now surplus to requirements: at best, they are seen as having become merely commercial representatives; at worst, they are considered redundant. This view is mistaken because there is more to international relations than commerce, and a body of (relatively independent) professional political analysts is vital to the furthering of a state's aims, whatever they are.

▶ The 'madness of sanity'

The argument so far has been that the international level of world politics is characterized by a culture of mistrust, but that co-operation is possible, and when 'enlightened self-interest' is involved such co-operation can be far-reaching (as in the growth of security communities). Collective action, nonetheless, can be acrimonious even when strong common interests are involved. This has been chronic in the case of 'burden sharing' within NATO: while all sign up to the principle rhetorically, in practice national self-interest quickly kicks in on all sides, as members try to have the benefit of collective defence while trying to minimize how much they contribute in money, equipment, personnel and especially blood. Overcoming the collective action problem is one that nation-states have always found difficult, even when it has made rational sense.

All might agree that sanity in human affairs would involve wholehearted co-operation between states, leading to disarmament, trade in pursuit of absolute gains for all, global justice, and working together to prevent or mitigate climate change, environmental destruction and other global challenges. From the political perspective of state leaders, however, committed by their roles to prioritize national self-interest, the international arena is one of competition over security, prosperity and national prestige. What therefore seems to be sanity from a collective human perspective can appear risky or even foolhardy from the perspective of a national player in the international power struggle.

International history is therefore full of unsuccessful negotiations, when governments have failed to agree to disarm, to bring an end to poverty, to help the weak, to decisively slow down climate change, to control nuclear weapons or to abolish war. The reason is simple. If national negotiators try too hard, and give away too much, or are too trusting, then their state may fall behind or lose out in the games of nations. In this situation, as Rousseau observed over two hundred years ago, 'to be sane in a world of madmen is itself a kind of madness'.

6

Political economy, capitalism, globalization

'We can't solve problems by using the same kind of thinking we used when we created them.'

Albert Einstein

Were a group of newspaper foreign correspondents to be resurrected from a century ago, when the academic study of IR began, they would find much that is familiar but plenty that would be mind-boggling. What was then far-fetched science fiction is today's strategic fact in the accuracy and destructiveness of modern weaponry, while today's dazzling information technology would leave them speechless, for a moment. Other changes, more directly political and economic, would be surprising but not as shocking. In particular, it would take time to understand the daily preoccupation of governments today with the global economy and the implications of globalization. International relations are a spicy brew comprising the ancient and the startlingly recent.

▶ It's the global political economy, stupid!

This subtitle is a variation on the phrase used in the 1992 US presidential campaign when Bill Clinton, the challenger, was told by an adviser what he must prioritize – the US economy – if he was to win. The message is similar for those wishing to understand international relations, though this time the focus must be the global economy. It is not the whole of the matter, but it is critical, and profoundly political.

In the eighteenth century the term 'political economy' embraced the trinity of economics (production), politics (ideologies and institutions) and moral philosophy (applied ethics). By the end of the following century the term had generally been shortened to 'economics', and so it has continued. The more scientific (that is, mathematical) the study of economics has become, the more, regrettably, it has been divorced from its political and ethical dimensions.

We do not have to be disciples of Karl Marx to appreciate the multi-dimensionality of economics. Note the world-views of the stridently un-Marxist Margaret Thatcher, and the remarkable diplomat with supranational vision Jean Monnet ('the father of Europe'). Thatcher understood the synergy of economics, politics and moral ends: 'If you change the approach [to economics],' she said, 'you really are after the heart and soul of the nation. Economics are the method; the object is to change the heart and soul.' Monnet, for his part, believed 'economics is a means to a political end' – in his case, the motor for European integration after the Second World War. Monnet said: 'Make men work together [and] show them that beyond their differences and geographical boundaries there lies a common interest.' Both Thatcher and Monnet understood that economics – its concepts and beliefs as well as its material forms – help create political reality.

One of the most persistent theories uniting economics, politics and moral ends in international relations is 'functionalism'. Its chief exponent was a Romanian-born theorist, David Mitrany, who in *A Working Peace System* (1943) and other writings proposed a bottom-up approach to building peace. His theory began with the simple idea that working together on common 'functional' projects across borders would reshape loyalties and strengthen the ties that bind people together. Later theorists developed functionalist notions as a way of promoting comprehensive international economic integration, particularly in Europe.

Functionalism stands apart from the dominant tradition of understanding economics in international relations. In this latter tradition, economics were primarily concerned with the exercise of state power and especially the accumulation of military potential. The most influential theory in this regard was 'mercantilism', which, between the sixteenth and eighteenth centuries, advocated building state power through the growth of economic strength at home and abroad by 'beggar-my-neighbour' policies in pursuit of favourable trade balances, wealth and war potential.

But economic strength is not only relevant to military and other forms of 'hard' power. 'Soft' power also depends upon the bottom line. US economic domination globally after the Second World War underpinned the Americanization of global culture, and thus the political leverage and economic advantages that follow from cultural domination. Language and material power have a dialectical relationship. Language is critical in the exercise of soft power, with those formerly local languages (like English) that become world languages doing so as a result of the economic might that fed and sustained successful armies and navies. Language followed the flag (itself a creation of language) and soft power built upon hard.

Despite the interconnectedness of economics and politics, the temptation to separate them has persisted. In academic IR, this traditionally took the form of distinguishing between 'high' and 'low' politics. Today, the resurrected foreign correspondents referred to earlier would discover that the distinction is being rubbed out, as are some of the boundaries between 'domestic' and 'foreign'. The boundaries are less dogmatically enforced because of the character of transnational commerce, as governments more than ever before must deliver on jobs and control taxes at home, while satisfying 'the market' and promoting exports abroad. If governments do not deliver, elections may be lost; and they will not deliver unless they succeed in the global economy.

How 'low' politics became 'high'

Defence and security issues were traditionally considered 'high' politics, whereas (domestic) economic and social matters were categorized as 'low'. As the threat of major war has declined, and governments have increasingly been seen as responsible for their people's welfare, their economic competence has risen in political significance. Jobs, tax arrangements, welfare policy, attitudes to immigration, business regulations, trade agreements, free-trade arrangements, regional and other economic regimes, and international relations now comprise a complex bundle of interrelated priorities for governments. Local has become global, global has become local, and low has become high.

A major consequence of the conceptual divorce between economics and politics has been the growth of the assumption that economic problems require technical ('economic') fixes, not political ones. The leadership of the Soviet Union, notably, took the opposite view after 1989: it accepted that economic progress depended on the most fundamental of all political fixes – that of ideological and state surrender.

Today, a narrow, technocratic, view of economics dominates the discourse of economics almost everywhere. This has been made to seem common sense by those defined as 'experts' on economics by the global media. Those thus selected to pronounce on economic matters are overwhelmingly insiders (analysts from the financial world, for example); their world-view and interest allow them only (technical) insider solutions to whatever is being discussed. But the global marketplace they inhabit is not a politics-free zone. It is not 'objective'. The technocratic solutions they recommend always have political consequences; they are only superficially economic fixes to economic problems. Meanwhile, outsider critics, with an eye to the wider implications of economics, are generally marginalized by the same global media. History is famously written by the winners, and the economic system that triumphed globally with the collapse of the Soviet empire is legitimized daily by its insider winners as the only economic game in town. We live at a time when economics is what its capitalist victors say it is.

▶ The triumph of neoliberalism?

The story of the triumph of capitalism is a long one. As influentially explained by the social theorist Immanuel

Wallerstein in his 'world-system theory', the story stretches back 700 years, beginning with the co-development of states and markets in Europe. Gradually, European imperialism, technological innovation, and the internationalization of capital incorporated hitherto largely self-sufficient countries into one world economy.

This story now appears inevitable, but it did not always – or even recently – seem so. In the twentieth century there was a persistent challenge to the onward march of capitalism by advocates of planned economies. The Soviet model, for many across the world, was once the future. Others toyed with the theory of 'convergence', the idea that there was a logic in the industrial and technological growth of modern states that would produce convergent political, economic and social structures. But convergence vanished, like other once-interesting theories. So did the Soviet Union, like other one-time superpowers. With the Soviet surrender to the global market in the late 1980s, and communist China's growing centrality to it through the 1990s, there now seems to be no workable alternative.

This rise and rise of capitalism had already been embedded in global (liberal economic) institutions after the Second World War. The 'Bretton Woods system', which took its name from the founding conference in New Hampshire in 1944, established a set of novel international monetary agreements and institutions: the World Bank (originally the International Bank for Reconstruction and Development) and the International Monetary Fund. These, together with the General Agreement on Tariffs and Trade in 1947 (which became the World Trade Organization after 1995), provided a multilateral framework of rules for the governance of the global economy under the political leadership of the United States and its liberal-democratic allies. As such, they were basic to the US-led political rebuilding and management of the post-war order. They were thought necessary not only to prevent another Great Depression like that which had contributed to the drift to war in the 1930s, but they also offered a liberal economic counter to the challenge of the Soviet model. With the end of the Cold War, the collapse of the Soviet alternative and the rise of newly powerful economies, the most significant bargaining table globally became the Group of Twenty (G-20), established in 1999. Russia and China joined this most exclusive of capitalist clubs.

Shutterstock

▲ Shanghai waterfront: will the yuan prove mightier than the sword?

The umbrella term 'capitalism', whether praised or pilloried, covers a variety of forms or cultures. The version that triumphed globally by the 1990s was 'neoliberalism'. While undoubtedly global, capitalism today also reflects national cultures: some capitalisms tend towards individualism, others to communitarianism, some to state capitalism and others still towards social democracy. These cultural tendencies are strengthened by the fact that the headquarters and majority benefits of global corporations remain nationally based.

Neoliberalism

By the 1980s the term 'neoliberalism' had come to embrace a distinct range of policies with profound political and social as well as economic consequences. Its 'economic' policy aims include moving towards deregulating markets and labour, privatizing state assets, reducing the state (including shrinking the public sector), and cutting public expenditure on social provision ('individual responsibility' rather than 'welfare'). For advocates of neoliberalism, the shrinking of the state and the freeing of enterprise were supposed to be in the interests of all, but the record has been different: unemployment, inequality and debt are widespread.

Nobody can doubt the triumph of neoliberal capitalism in an empirical sense, but, as has been stressed, there is more to economics than economic policy. A balance sheet of the successes and failures of the 'triumph of capitalism' presents a complex picture, and one's assessment of the bottom line will depend largely on one's views about its political and moral dimensions.

Capitalism's cheerleaders can point to various successes over recent decades. Above all, it is claimed that neoliberalism's triumph has brought millions out of absolute poverty across the world. As a result of increased levels of prosperity, life opportunities have expanded. In particular, remarkable numbers of people in Asia have been lifted into the middle class. It is also claimed that success can be measured by rising employment and improved working standards – both said to be encouraged by a weakening of trade unions. Capitalism shows its genius by giving people what it persuades them they need, and builds a world of greater choice and 'smaller' states (in an economic sense).

These views are misleading in the opinion of critics of neoliberalism. Instead, they stress that some of its supposed successes merely exacerbate fundamental national and global problems. The greater the size of the global middle class, for example, the greater the exploitation of the natural environment in order to provide more food (especially meat) and service other desires (notably tourism). Negative environmental impacts (the destruction of natural habitat and the increase in pollution) should be of grave concern, but are generally marginalized as capitalism's 'externalities'; that is, they are the costs that nobody chooses, and nobody directly pays for in the short run, but which are a price all will have to bear, sometime. Critics also point to more directly political failures resulting from the spread of neoliberalism, especially the widening of inequality with all its regressive consequences. And while the international super-rich flaunt their excesses, countless millions struggle to survive, as 'structural adjustment' disciplines and 'predatory global corporations' in recent decades have squeezed developing countries. The first commandment of neoliberalism is 'growth' as measured by metrics such as GDP (gross domestic product), but the global GDP league tables that drive policies tell us little about the lives of real people in real places.

As the number of economists and the sophistication of economic models grow apace, periodic crises of capitalism have not been avoided. The association of 'mature economies' with 'financialization' helped cause the massive 1997 Asian crisis, sparked by the financial collapse in Thailand, and the global financial crisis of 2007–09, sparked by speculation in housing in the United States. Such crises shatter the lives of millions through unemployment and insecurity. Yet these are the 'ordinary workings of capitalism' in the authoritative words of Paul Volker, former chair of the US Federal Reserve.

The global winners do well, but even here there is a dark side. Possessive individualism, cultivated by capitalism, has resulted in what the economist Kenneth J. Galbraith in the 1990s called a 'culture of contentment'. By this he meant that a wealthy class had arisen across the developed world completely tied up in the furthering of its own interests. Its members voted for those parties promising to further their interests, especially by reducing taxes. As the contented class consolidated, a permanent underclass developed, and the idea of economic justice, locally and globally, went absent without leave. According to economic historian Robert

Heilbronner, this 'divine right of the consumer' stores up great problems for the future.

Capitalism creates winners and losers and, as it does so, intrudes into all levels of human relations. If the dominating logic of anarchy described in Chapter 1 leads to competition between states for security and power, the logic of capitalism promotes competition between states for prosperity and power. In October 2013 UK Prime Minister David Cameron could have been speaking for the leaders of all countries trapped in their own politico-economic hour of reckoning when he declared: 'We're in a global race today and that means an hour of reckoning for countries like ours. Sink or swim. Do or decline.'

Without doubt, the capitalist culture of neoliberalism has triumphed. The question is: can the world, human and non-human, afford it?

▶ Globalization and its discontents

The growth of the global economy has been a powerful engine behind the image and reality of today's 'shrinking world'. In the final quarter of the twentieth century it became commonplace to hear about 'the global village', 'the global neighbourhood', the 'borderless world' and the '24/7' interconnected planet. The processes that helped bring about such images have been part of the human story for millennia – trade, exploration, technological innovation and political expansion – but only in recent decades has it been possible to conceptualize 'human society' as a global entity. The controversial term 'globalization' attempts to capture this.

Globalization is a historic step-change (like the Industrial Revolution) that has altered the world for ever. It describes the radical growth and densification of interrelationships globally, impacting on traditional conceptions of time, space and boundaries – and hence on culture, identity and politics. It can be understood as both a process and a project.

As a process, globalization is synonymous with the shrinking of space and time through the revolution in technology symbolized by jumbo jets and the Internet. As a project, it refers to the spread and triumph of neoliberal capitalism. Over a remarkably short span of several decades, process and project together have brought about spectacular changes in the daily life of the planet. These include instantaneous communication across continents, the transnational organization of production ('deterritorialization'), the 24-hour global financial system, and changing consumption patterns and expectations. The material changes are revolutionary, but so, too, are the implications for family, social and political relations. Economics, as suggested earlier, is politics and morality by other means.

Not surprisingly, many exaggerate the extent of the step-change, and there are profound disagreements about its consequences. To 'hyper-globalizers' its momentum is unstoppable and almost wholly positive: easier access and communication across borders promote positive relations; the prospect arises of increased prosperity and liberal lifestyles for all; there is promise of better education, jobs and opportunities; improved standards (from toilets to worker regulations) have spread; and a networked and harmonious world society is in sight. Against this largely top-down view, 'anti-globalizers' stress what they regard as the negative consequences of globalization: the homogenization of culture leading to identity crises; lifestyle conformism resulting in 'globesity' and the eradication of diversity; the growth of inequality; domination and exploitation by unelected and unaccountable multinational corporations; increasingly intrusive national and global surveillance; entanglement in a global financial system subject to periodic collapses; insecurity and conflict; and radical transformations under nobody's control.

The balance sheet of globalization is complex, but the extent of the change has not always been as radical as some argue. Much remains the same. We do not live in a 'post-international' or 'borderless' world. To suggest this would be an insult to the 366 individuals who drowned off the island of Lampedusa in October 2013 seeking to enter the EU, not to mention the 'boat people' shipped on by the Australian government to Papua New Guinea. Borders matter, and for many the matter is life or death.

Globalization has been uneven in its impact. As the old adage has it, for some (the wealthy) the world is now their village, but for many (the poor) their village is still their world. Though fewer people live in absolute poverty, inequalities have generally increased. More positively, however, the threat of homogenization has been met by the growth of cultural hybrids, the flowering of local cultures, and a wider appreciation of the local. Globalization creates a 'global-we' in the sense of a community of fate, thrown closer together on a shrinking planet; but we still experience it very differently. We are discovering that neither 'global village' nor 'global neighbourhood' are necessarily cosy images: they contain all the paradoxes of proximity.

Without doubt, the processes of globalization will continue as technology develops: time and space will shrink. But what of globalization as a project? In 2001 the radical development economist Susan George surprised her anti-globalization audience by declaring: 'We are "pro-globalization.' She proceeded to argue that 'we are in favour of sharing friendship, culture, cooking, solidarity, wealth and resources' across the world. What matters is not 'globalization' as a process, she was implying, but its character as a project.

7

Values, ethics, choices

'You're all the same, you intellectuals: everything is cracking and collapsing, the guns are on the point of going off, and you stand there calmly claiming the right to be convinced.'

'Brunet' (in Jean-Paul Sartre, The Age of Reason)

At the end of the Cold War film *Fail-Safe* – a nicely ironic title – the US President orders his old air-force friend to drop two 20-megaton bombs on New York City, where both their wives happen to be, as well as millions of other fellow Americans. A catastrophic technical malfunction had resulted in a US bomber attacking and destroying Moscow, and Soviet nuclear forces were primed for instant retaliation. The President hoped that an act of self-sacrifice against New York would succeed as a supremely costly signal of common humanity to the Soviet leader, and so prevent the escalatory logic of mutual assured destruction (MAD) leading to the wiping out of both societies. Earlier, one of the President's advisers, 'Professor Groteschele', had shown impeccable personal morality (as a married man) by rejecting the escalatory advances of an attractive woman. Yet, when it came to morality in the realm of international relations, his advice to the President was that the United States should go all the way, whatever the cost, and take the opportunity created by the technical malfunction to screw the Soviet communists once and for all. This would be the ultimate 'wargasm', to use a coining of Herman Kahn, a controversial US nuclear strategist of the time, and possibly the real-life model for Groteschele.

The scenario played out in *Fail-Safe* was fiction but by no means 'thinking the unthinkable' – another term popularized by Kahn. Nuclear war-gamers played, and for sure still play, many unlikely scenarios, while international history over the centuries has thrown up numerous unthought crises (moments of danger/ moments of opportunity). Who could have predicted the chain of decision-making that led from the assassination of Archduke Franz Ferdinand by a Serbian nationalist on 28 June 1914 into a world war of continuing historical significance?

The study of IR is sometimes understood as the study of power: it can equally be understood as the examination of people making the toughest calls on the biggest political stage. These calls reveal international relations not as an amoral activity but as an arena of values (coming from religion, reason, culture, political ideology or whatever), ethics (standards of right and wrong) and choices (even if very limited ones, and ones with only bad outcomes). IR is a landscape of ethics, and for realists as much as for anybody else.

▶ The ethics of responsibility

The *Fail-Safe* fictional scenario illustrates what is known as the 'ethics of responsibility'. A key thinker here was the German sociologist Max Weber (1864–1920), who argued that clean hands were not an option in the turbulent and competitive arena of politics. What matters is how politicians conduct themselves under the burden of responsibility. This means giving due consideration to all relevant matters (evidence, moral dimensions, ultimate ends) and then coming to a decision with as much objectivity as possible.

When faced by situations in which there seems no prospect of a positive outcome, whatever one decides, people are drawn in their personal lives to the 'principle of the lesser evil' for guidance. It is a simple idea, and for many is intuitive. Confronted by several options, each of which threatens a negative outcome ('evil' is used loosely in this context), one chooses the course that seems least dangerous, least costly or least likely to cause harm. When translated into the international arena, the options facing decision-makers sometimes have 'the fate of nations' written across them. Should military intervention for humanitarian purposes be undertaken when the outcome will always be uncertain in terms of casualties and success? But can non-intervention be justifiable, when there is the certain knowledge that a violent humanitarian emergency will continue, and possibly get worse? How should foreign aid given to impoverished countries be balanced against welfare spending at home? At the sharp end, IR is the study of applied ethics.

The Syrian imbroglio

The situation in Syria after 2011 developed from a peaceful protest to a bloody civil war that drew in outsiders and spilled over borders. Parallels were drawn with 1914. For all concerned, it is a case study in the ethics of responsibility.

As soon as the imbroglio moved beyond the prospect of peaceful negotiations between the protesters and the regime, there would be no good outcomes. The situation deteriorated alongside a fearful increase in violence, an unwillingness among the key players to compromise, growing involvement by external forces, escalating sectarian strife within Syrian society, and the piteous suffering of frightened people. Whatever any outside government chose to do, no ethically uncompromised position was available. No policy (including non-intervention) was without impact on Syria's battlefields, and every military option involved risk and loss. A pacifist but interventionist position, offering humanitarian help only, would not stop the bodies piling up as long as the warring parties continued to put their hopes in violence as 'a continuation of politics'.

International history throws up many occasions when the ethics of responsibility have placed the fate of millions on the single decision of a political leader. On 5 June 1944 General Dwight D. Eisenhower, pressurized by time and uncertain weather, decided to launch Operation Overlord against Nazi-occupied Europe (having a note in his pocket accepting all blame if the operation failed); on 25 July 1945 President Harry S. Truman wrote in his diary that he had taken the decision to use the atomic bomb on Japan, and later defined his role as President in relation to the famous motto on his desktop, 'The buck stops here'; through the 13 days of the Cuban Missile Crisis in October 1962, President Kennedy and Premier Khrushchev went 'eyeball to eyeball', balancing the assertion of their national interests against the future of civilized life in the northern hemisphere; and in 1989 General Secretary Gorbachev was faced with the dangers involved in using force to maintain the Soviet empire in eastern Europe, or losing it through the 'Sinatra doctrine' (allowing the states concerned to do it 'their way'). These were some of international history's iconic moments, but the ethics of responsibility invariably confront decision-makers each time they turn up for work.

Values, ethics and choices in this chapter so far have focused on governments, but the normative dimensions of international relations reach beyond decision-makers and the fate of nations. Ethics go all the way down. Individuals have become increasingly significant in international relations, with the horrendous history of human wrongs leading to the rise of human rights.

▶ Individuals matter

The idea of humans having rights goes back almost 4,000 years, to when the Babylonian King Hammurabi decreed laws requiring that charges against a person needed to be proved in court. Human rights, broadly conceived, are not therefore, as some critics maintain, a recent invention of 'the West' simply imposed on 'the rest'.

Through the 40 centuries since Hammurabi, ideas about rights have varied widely, as has the consistency of their application. That noted, the general direction has been towards a widening of standard-setting, the embedding of rights thinking, and the clarification of the obligations of states towards their citizens and of individuals towards society and one another. Historically, this expansion of rights within countries extended group by group (for instance, from 'freemen' to property owners to all males). In the eighteenth century the idea of human emancipation was universalized by the Enlightenment.

The long journey of human rights reached its most decisive international milestone in 1948, with the adoption by the UN General Assembly of the Universal Declaration of Human Rights (UDHR). Its Preamble declares the 'recognition of the inherent dignity and of the equal and inalienable rights of all members of the human family', and its articles offer comprehensive rights to all. The Declaration was endorsed by the overwhelming majority of states at the time, and its principles continue to be cited by governments, legal organizations and civil society globally when rights are threatened or denied.

Many criticisms have been levelled against the human rights culture that developed after 1948. One of the commonest, hinted at above, is the alleged Western bias in human rights policies. This issue has occasionally been politically prominent, as with the heated debate in the 1990s about 'Asian' values, when the leaders of China, Malaysia and Singapore in particular asserted that their human rights values derived from different cultures and histories from those of the Western states in the forefront of the universal human rights project. It was argued, for example, that 'Asian' values of community, respect, social harmony and authority clashed with 'Western' values of individualism, dissent, free speech, democratic diversity and liberal democracy. Critics of the 'Asian values' position argued that values across Asia are varied (as are so-called 'Western' values), while the main function of the 'Asian values' rhetoric was to entrench the power of authoritarian elites in Asian countries. At issue in all such discussions is the vexed matter of 'cultural relativism'.

Cultural relativism

Cultural relativism is the view that each 'culture' possesses a coherent set of values and customs. Relativists argue that it is only in its own – and not universal – terms that one can properly interpret the attitudes and behaviour of any society or culture. The main counters to the relativist position are: it exaggerates the self-contained character of societies and cultures; if one believes cultures are unique and mutually incomprehensible, then the basis for comparison and indeed mutual understanding is undermined; cultural relativism leads to 'moral relativism', which can lead to accepting cruelty in the name of local traditions and values; there is a great deal of cross-cultural consensus on values, including, notably, between major religions; and deference to cultural relativism privileges the most conservative elements in any society, and especially patriarchal elites.

Relativism and universalism serve different roles. When making anthropological observations, it is desirable to be sensitive to cultural relativism, showing acute awareness of local particularities. Consideration of human rights is a different activity. Here, what matters is that each of us is related to everybody else not only as biological beings, but through our common experience as children, brothers or sisters, parents, friends, gendered bodies, and the rest. We are humans first, so why should 'culture' be given the last word?

The criticisms of the human rights regime goes beyond its supposed universalism. Some ethicists question the 'rights obsession' of our times, arguing that other values such as kindness are more important. But why must there be a choice? Why not promote kindness *and* rights? Other philosophers argue that rights are mere 'superstitions'. But we know that ideas (in this case, entitlements) are at the heart of all structures of human social existence. In this sense, human rights are as real as democracy. A final criticism – going back before the 9/11 attacks on New York, but intensified after them – is that the post-1948 human rights regime has been in decline in face of the assertiveness of non- (and anti-) Western voices.

Without doubt, the effectiveness of the universal human rights regime fluctuates, but the project seems secure. This is evident in the popular claims for democracy in Burma in recent decades in face of violent crackdowns by the military regime; in the emancipatory energy behind the Arab Revolutions, even if 'Spring' has turned to 'Winter'; and in the challenges to tyranny at the risk of imprisonment or death faced by journalists and protesters in Putin's Russia. The human rights project will surely outlive the 'midlife crisis' Michael Ignatieff warned of as long ago as 1999. Yet *nowhere* can human rights be taken for granted. The torture, rendition and other abuses of human rights that accompanied the prosecution of the US 'Global War on Terror' show how standards can slip. What has been won can be lost.

Although the record of human rights implementation over the decades has varied enormously, the UDHR gave humankind a common language for talking about rights, even if the words sometimes mean different things. In this regard, the very hypocrisy of governments revealed in the gap between their words and actions shows the homage that vice sometimes pays to virtue. Even hypocrisy can represent a kind of global moral progress. At best, human rights norms improve not only the lives of individuals and groups, but are of progressive geopolitical significance. The human rights dimensions of the Helsinki Final Act of 1975, for example, contributed decisively to the peaceful endings of the Cold War. In different ways, the condition of human rights globally reveals something important about the state of humanity.

▶ Worlds in collision?

If there is one thing the human species has learned in its five- to six-million-year journey since hominids separated from apes, it has been how to divide ourselves from one other: into genders, tribes, classes, empires, religions, civilizations, states, nations, races and all the other inventive ways of splitting the species. These divisions, inventions of the human mind over time, make the politics of identity one of the most perplexing issues in international relations.

'Identity' is the complex of feelings, ideas and thoughts comprising the self-image of an individual or group; it is how an individual or group hopes to be seen by others, and then is perceived and labelled by them. In international relations, the most politically significant identity since the end of the eighteenth century has been *the nation*, with its ethnic, religious and cultural associations, and political expression in nationalism.

'Nations' are not natural phenomena: they are not primordial social entities. They are inventions of the mind that have been constructed and perpetuated through the ideas, institutions and routines that carry them forward. For several hundred years humans have been nationalized almost from birth through sophisticated and not so sophisticated socialization processes; these processes continue, with more or less success, throughout life. The modern notion of the nation that arose in Europe is now virtually universal. The national idea dominates, even where the 'tribe' may be the primary daily marker of identity. Other significant markers serving as referents for values, morality and ethics include 'religion', 'civilization', 'common humanity', 'class' and 'gender'. Scare quotes are put around these words to underline that identities are ideas developed through history, not brandings from the beginning of time.

The various identities just listed are frequently classified by IR scholars in relation to two approaches to global living: 'communitarian' and 'cosmopolitan'. The values and impulses of the former have dominated through recorded history, but the latter has rarely been absent.

Definitions

Communitarianism is the claim that political and ethical positions can be properly understood only in relation to distinct cultural, ethnic and political communities. For realists, above all, the state is asserted as having primacy as the source and arbiter of ethical positions. 'Universalist' ideas are rejected as being top-down.

Cosmopolitanism (the idea of being a world citizen) is the claim that all humans are equal, and that political and cultural boundaries have no moral standing. Whether and to what extent this requires that common humanity must have common political institutions (ultimately a central world government) is something over which cosmopolitans disagree.

The communitarian approach focuses on difference. Towards the extreme end of this spectrum, it is claimed that ethical systems are mutually exclusive: the technical term for this is 'incommensurability'. This implies that different thoughtways, paradigms and theories do not simply look at the same world from a different perspective, but that they see a different world. This view was popularized through the 1990s by Huntington's 'Clash of Civilizations' thesis (see Chapter 3). It was contested by, among others, Edward Said, who commented that the challenge globally is not a clash of civilizations, but a 'Clash of Ignorance'.

For Huntington and his followers, religion is central to the idea of a civilization. Long thought to have been of declining significance in international relations, religion since the 1970s has become increasingly prominent, not least because of the widespread association of religion with terrorism.

When considering the place of religion in international relations, four oversimplifications should be avoided:

1 *The complete separation of 'religion' and 'politics'.* To think a complete distinction is possible involves a particular understanding of the world, namely the secular

outlook that developed in Europe from the Reformation onwards. Politics in some societies, like the rest of life, is a religious experience; it is not something separate.

2 *The assumption that there must be one truly authentic religious view on each political issue.* If life is a religious experience, so are parts of it: 'Islamic terrorism' is a religious experience for jihadists, just as 'Christian terrorism' can be in Ireland and elsewhere. History graphically records how contested the authentic voice has been in religion. In politics, religion is what people say and do.

3 *The tendency to impose 'solitarist' identities.* Amartya Sen coined the term 'solitarist' to challenge the familiar mindset consigning people to one all-encompassing identity. There is more to a religion than its conventional label, and more to people than their religion: religions have sub-divisions and humans have multiple identities. How religious, national, class, gender and other affiliations are balanced and play out in particular political situations will vary. It was misleading, therefore – albeit tempting – to interpret protest in Turkey in 2013 as simply 'secularist' versus 'Islamist', or in Syria as simply 'sectarian', between Sunni and Shi'a.

4 *The incompatibility in the political realm of secular ideas and religion.* Many societies are becoming more mixed and their public spaces increasingly multi-religious. Sen has pointed to two inspiring leaders as examples of how to interact harmoniously in such circumstances: the Buddhist Emperor Ashoka in India in the third century BCE, and the Mughal Emperor Akbar at the end of the sixteenth century CE. The

former set down rules for dialogue across difference, and the latter defended the idea of the state being separate from different religions in the interest of general toleration.

Reason and harmony point to religion (in the sense of institutions and their differences over the origins of Truth) being kept out of political public space, though not the humane values embedded in and cherished by people of faith. In globalized times, people must reason together by focusing on values all can understand and share, and therefore over which all can reasonably argue, rather than traditions and ultimate beliefs that most do not understand and cannot share.

▶ Negotiating diversity

Can there ever be harmony in a world that is a multinational, multi-religious, multicultural, multiracial and multi-ethnic kaleidoscope – all in motion in a multi-state system characterized by an uneven distribution of resources, power and potential? The odds are not promising. But there is reason for hope, and how we act collectively will shape the outcome: fatalism would be self-fulfilling.

First, human society globally is rapidly becoming a community of fate, as we face common threats in a shrinking planet. Common interests point to 'one worldist' perspectives being increasingly realistic.

Second, the gathering pace of global common interests converges with the tradition going back to the 'world citizen' sensibility of the Stoics in ancient Greece. Such an outlook is alive today in global civil society's activism on behalf of human rights, economic justice, the control and abolition of nuclear weapons, environmental sustainability and peace.

Third, there is growing institutionalization (governance) across borders. The role played by international law is part of this, and its daily effectiveness in the life of the world is sometimes underestimated. Institutionalization at the state level is often a matter of converging material interests, as in trade agreements, but it is sometimes inspired by common humanity ideals. The latter was

TJeerd Royaards/Cartoon Movement

▲ 'Food Crisis? What Food Crisis?' by Tjeerd Royaards (August 2012). This cartoon was provoked by fears of a global food crisis brought on, in part, by the effects of the lengthy drought on US corn crops. As ever, the impact of such a crisis was expected to be most devastating to the poor of the world.

evident in the adoption in 1994 of the UNDP's 'human security' agenda, and in the endorsing in 2005 by the UN's World Summit of the norm of 'Responsibility to Protect'. Here, common humanity impulses were revealed at the heart of the world's only multi-functional and near-universal international organization, however limited the practical follow-up.

The focus on discord at the international level in much of this book has been justifiable in relation to the way the most powerful states have behaved through much of history. That noted, the desire for and the achievement of harmony have never been entirely absent. As peace researchers insist, the historical record reveals former enemies reconciling, predictable peace existing between some states, the persistence of justice in international discourse, lengthy periods of coexistence between some races and religions and cultures, conflict prevention techniques being employed, and the expansion of 'imagined communities' beyond the local neighbourhood. In these ways, the dynamics of a better world are immanent in human history. But how are they to be brought out?

1 *Aim for 'hospitality', not love.* To love all humanity is too grandiose an aim when it seems impossible in one's own street. However, treating others with 'hospitality', as one would hope to be treated oneself, is practical and rational and the basis for Kant's notion of 'world citizenship'. But even this is beyond some governments, societies and individuals. The inhospitability sometimes shown towards migrants

and refugees is a measure of how far international society has yet to go.

2 *Focus on values, not ultimate beliefs.* When cultures clash, the prospects for harmonious coexistence are improved if a dialogue of values is engaged, and not an argument about basic beliefs (such as the religious foundations of Truth). Rational discussion is possible about cruelty, crime, family values, peace, justice and so on, without recourse to the ultimate ethical foundations of ideas. By focusing on the possibility of shared values rather than on incommensurable religious or non-religious beliefs, it should be possible to question specific behaviour, such as terrorism, without becoming embroiled in a fundamental cultural/religious confrontation.

3 *Resist labelling.* Those seeking to contribute to a more harmonious world must avoid what Sen calls 'the miniaturization of human beings' by 'solitarist' labelling. Miniaturization involves avoiding 'one allegedly dominant system' of classifying a person, be it by religion or community. Terrorists miniaturize, and their victims respond, in turn, by counter-miniaturizing. Coexistence requires exploring the complexities of identity by looking for the person behind the label.

4 *Prioritize the future over the past.* Ours is not the best of all possible worlds, and business as usual will not work. We must therefore look towards global governance, *if not beyond to actual government*, for the implementation of what is needed in face of global

challenges. Thinking identities forward must be part of this, as opposed to embracing and consolidating old myths. The situation requires the imagining and cultivation of new identities, responding to the changing realities of global life.

Confronted by all the inherited problems of the past, and the multiplying challenges of the future, it is easy for individuals to succumb to a sense of hopelessness and helplessness about international relations. What can one person do? To succumb to this way of thinking would be a mistake, for the progressive things in political life – democratic elections, the rule of law, human rights, international organizations committed to peace – are the result of individuals joining together and choosing to try to change one reality for a better one.

Though we all have very different levels of responsibility and power, each one of us is confronted by daily dilemmas with international implications: Which political party deserves my vote on its foreign and defence policy? How much money (if any) should I contribute to charities working on international development or human rights? Why should I donate money to help alleviate the suffering of strangers in strange lands when locals need help? International relations are not just for governments. Arguing the world begins at home.

8

Inventing humanity

'... in forging a world in which "humanity" has become a pragmatic reality with a common destiny, we do not arrive at the end of history. World history has just begun.'

Michael Geyer and Charles Bright

'Pessimists don't build gas chambers.' This opinion, given by Shalom Auslander to a character in his 2012 novel *Hope: A Tragedy*, was a warning against the excesses of political optimism: he was telling us to beware those who believe that what they want to happen is bound to happen. Conviction about the future can be dangerous to all around.

Translated into international relations, this is a warning against those convinced that utopia is on the horizon, the 'city upon a hill' is in sight, 'New Jerusalem' is around the corner, or the 'promised land' will be perfect. Those with such convictions can be tempted into believing that the (glorious and inevitable) end point will justify whatever means, whatever risks, whatever costs, and whatever dirty hands are thought necessary to give history a push. When optimism, power and the will to win converge with opportunity, the outcome may be catastrophic. Recall the ruthless determination of those believing in communism's inevitable victory, or the horrific racial exterminism of the Nazis.

▶ No country for optimists

It was argued in the previous chapter that hope can be rational in international relations. It can only be rational, however, if it is based on a realistic analysis of the workings of the international system. This is why I have emphasized the competitive 'texture' (see Chapter 1) of the international system. Giving due attention to the stubborn structures and traditional norms of international relations discourages irrelevance and unrealism.

Previous chapters have offered glimpses of possibilities for change – even the rational hope for progressive change – and of the potentialities for positive agency by governments and individuals. While it has been made clear why virtues within domestic society – friendship, trust, truth-telling and non-violence – do not translate easily or ever into traditionally practised international relations, peaceful potentialities nevertheless exist, as was made evident in Chapter 7. If something has been possible in the past, Boulding used to argue, 'it is possible' again. But comprehensive radical change is unlikely as long as the dominant global mindset about the political organization of the world is characterized by statist priorities. What is more, this dominant mindset over the past few centuries is now startlingly at odds with the material dynamics and moral demands of a shrinking world in which millions of humans live desperate lives, and the natural world is being destroyed.

Humanity has been invented and reinvented through history. By 'humanity' here I do not mean simply our biological categorization as featherless bipeds. Rather, I refer to the *condition* or *quality* of being human, and my claim is that international relations are critical to what happens next: how we choose to exist together on the biggest political stage will decisively affect what becomes of all of us, everywhere. The mindset that dominates the international will draw up the plans and prepare the scaffolding for future humanity. We have humanities inside us: but which will we set free?

A discussion about international relations today is directly or indirectly an intervention in a debate about the future condition and quality of humanity. As we analyse sovereignty, political violence, global governance, communitarian and cosmopolitan ethics, interstate norms, policy instruments, institutions, agency and so on, we are not simply 'doing' current affairs; we are contributing to replicating or reconceiving humanity. The invention of 'crimes against humanity' is one illustration of what this can mean.

▶ Unfolding stories

The discussion of international relations in the years to come will focus on the following matters, singly or in combination.

Stories of sovereignty

Sovereignty will remain a controversial focus of attention. 'Who rules?' will run through every story. Sometimes it will be a case of undermining the symbol of Westphalia; at other times it will be in its honour. In the forefront of the former will be global market forces and international standards of behaviour, while struggles *for* sovereignty will take the form either of the breaking up of a particular state from within (as happened with Sudan in 2011), or from without (as happened with Crimea in 2014, and possibly other parts of Ukraine), or attempts to overthrow one regime by another (Syria since 2011). Extreme violence is always a possibility in these cases.

While the modalities of sovereign control continue to develop under globalization and transnational institutionalization (such as the EU), the symbol of national sovereignty remains compelling; the BRICs are among Westphalia's biggest supporters. Furthermore, the tides of globalization, instead of washing away the state, might well provoke higher defences, as nationalist flag-wavers demand the exclusion of outsiders to protect the way of life of those who feel historically entitled to their homeland.

Predictably, a patchwork of non-sovereign authorities will superimpose themselves on the Westphalian patchwork, and the interplay between them will decide whether the international level of world politics maintains or loses its historic 'causal weight' in shaping who gets what, when, where and how. If the historic statist/nationalist/international level maintains its domineering weight, it is difficult to see how global challenges to humanity and nature will be overcome.

Stories of identity

As ever, the character of particular states will be shaped by history, geography, power, ideology and the dominant population's sense of identity. Who are we?

As a result, states may take on the character of anything from a militarized 'garrison state' to a proponent of 'cosmopolitan democracy'. A common view is that religion will become an evermore significant factor in state development, and in this regard the Sunni/Shi'a divide is increasingly posited as a cause of future conflict in the Middle East, comparable to that between different types of Christianity in bygone Europe. A counter-view emphasizes the importance everywhere of pragmatic interests and national loyalties, and argues that these will count for more than religion at the end of the day. Others say that the gap between rich and poor remains the most decisive badge of identity globally and will provoke the building of 'gated communities' within and between states. Alongside these divisive identities will be stories of global civil society struggling to strengthen cosmopolitan bonds and institutions.

The identities that predominate will affect the character of states, and the character of states will affect the character of anarchy. In turn, the character of anarchy will shape the conditions of possibility for humanity as a whole.

Stories of hierarchy

If 'who will rule?' will headline national stories, the international equivalent will be 'who will dominate?' Since the Second World War the role of hegemon in global economic and military affairs has been the United States. 'Will this be another American century?' people will continue to ask until the answer becomes obvious; this may take longer than critics of the United States imagine. The manner in which US governments have played their hegemonic role has attracted great criticism over the decades, but would China (or India or a multipolar combination of states) do better? Will the global decline of the United States – if it is to be –

become a lesson about being careful about what one might wish for? Stories of hierarchy, for the foreseeable future, will be stories ending in question marks.

Hegemony

Hegemony refers to the authority a state is able to exercise over a region or globally. Imperial power implies coercive control. A hegemon, while possessing dominant power, exerts its influence by creating the rules that legitimize its leadership in institutions and by exercising ideological authority. 'Hegemonic stability' requires that the leaders of a dominant state possess the will and capability to be the international stabilizer of last resort – politically, economically and, ultimately, militarily. Supporters of the United States during the presidency of Barack Obama have worried that this role has been underplayed and that it might become a permanent and unfortunate habit.

Stories of war and rumours of war

Issues of hierarchy between great powers were traditionally sorted out by war. How this will be done in an age when war between leading industrial powers is thought unlikely remains to be discovered. Statistics point to the decline of major war, but levels of militarization across the world remain conspicuous, the risk of terrorism is high in some countries, and politically motivated violence is widespread.

There remain plentiful causes for future conflict: the escalation of security dilemmas cannot be ruled out, arising from strategic tinderboxes in East Asia and elsewhere, or from growing tensions over nuclear weapons proliferation; nor might the causes of old wars be avoided in new times, over natural resources such as energy and water. There is also the possibility of the further rise of what Mary Kaldor, global governance specialist, calls 'new wars'. These are complex conflicts with internal and external dimensions, where politics, crime and business interact, in which the intensity of violence may be low though the level of casualties is high. If people choose to fight, for whatever reason, the institutions to stop them, so far, remain weak.

Stories of revolt and revolution

Provoked by feelings of local and global injustice, a wave of dissent has spread, with networking assisted by the diffusion of social media. Politics are said to be shifting 'from below' in many parts of the world: demonstrations against authoritarian behaviour by governments have taken place in the heart of such cities as Cairo, Istanbul, Rio and Kiev; 'Occupy' actions against inequality sprang up in Madrid, London and New York; and the 'Arab Spring' and the Ukraine-Russia confrontation showed how such upsurges could easily spill across borders.

Where will such turmoil end? Is the talk of 'new politics' just talk? Might new or better democracies emerge? What about better international relations? Will transparency grow through 'citizen journalism' and whistle-blowing? What hope is there for a 'new economics' to develop? How will 'the people' successfully challenge established structures? Can we learn to stop the escalator that sometimes leads from peaceful protest to civil war to international crises or worse? Instead of new politics, how likely is it that established power structures will regroup, reorganize and return? Might the latest technology assist old politics more than the new? Revolution might be back, but Realpolitik never left.

Stories of governance

A traditional problem in international relations has been that of collective decision-making. The prioritizing of short-term self-interested gains before collective long-term interests is now of enhanced significance as a result of growing awareness of common (global) threats. The UN will be at the heart of many stories of attempts at collective international action, but it remains a club of states, not of 'we the peoples' as stated in the Preamble to the UN Charter. Tellingly, none of the UN's Millennium Goals (on primary education, poverty and so on, with a target date of 2015) has yet been achieved. Global governance is failing to rise to the challenges of the times. The obstacles are familiar: historic structures, selfish outlooks, mistrust and a distressing absence of world leaders with stature and vision.

Stories of nature

The absence of great world leaders, if this turns out to be the case, might come to be felt most dramatically in stories relating to the natural world, for the interplay between the traditional difficulties of collective action, the impact of exploitative capitalism on the environment, and the two billion or more increase in the global population over the coming decades may become the biggest story of the century. At the centre of this mix, but not by any means the whole of the problem, is coming climate change (or, more accurately, 'climate chaos'). The case for human responsibility for 'global warming' is increasingly persuasive, and in any event prudence should tell governments that they must act as though it were correct.

Mikhail Zlatovsky

▲ 'Coat Star' by Mikhail Zlatovsky – winner of first prize in the Ken Sprague Fund cartoon competition (2008) on global warming. The judges thought the image 'captured the shabbiness and sleazy way our planet is being devastated'.

Collective actions that might make a significant difference to the future of the planet move so slowly that markets stay confident that they can gamble on business as usual. While governments fiddle as the world heats up, climate change deniers remain confident about dismissing the increasingly undeniable. Failure to mitigate climate change increases the risks of political turmoil, mass migration, economic distress, food insecurity and violent conflict. Faced with these challenges, we cannot even take dismal comfort from the old line that 'things will have to get much worse before they get better': by the time they are much worse, a calamitous environmental momentum may have been set in place.

Stories of political economy

Just as neoliberal capitalism was coming to look unstoppable, its triumph appears to be a pyrrhic victory to a growing body of opinion, including, in 2013, the new Pope and the new leader of the Anglican Church. While we wait to see the outcome of the struggle between the clergy and capitalism, and between capitalism and nature, there are many other stories. Will emerging economies (Brazil, Russia, India) join China to dominate capitalism's most exclusive clubs, and so reshape political as well as economic trends? If the success of the Chinese model continues, will other aspiring powers learn that democracy is a luxury they cannot afford? Can the 'ordinary workings' of capitalism (including periodic transcontinental crises) be reformed? Might global capitalism become fairer to the developing world? Can governments in liberal democracies be re-elected if they fail to pander to possessive individualism? And, finally, returning to the fundamentals of political economy, is it not past the time for each of us to turn Thatcher's syllogism on its head, and argue that it is not for economics to change people, but for people to change economics in the human interest?

Stories of emancipation

Struggles for human emancipation are being played out daily across the world and focus particularly on the agendas proclaimed by global civil society: peace, justice, democracy, environmental sustainability, disarmament, the rule of law and an end to poverty. In some states, these hopes are being met by repression; in others, there are green shoots of expectation. The nuclear revolution opened up states to one sort of vulnerability; globalization has opened them up to many more.

Stories of emancipation will often develop in the vulnerabilities and potentialities arising from the interpenetration of the local and global. Security under these conditions requires the spread of human solidarity, and the provision of material necessities, access to knowledge, and freedom from direct and structural tyranny. Only upon a stronger and more emancipated global community can more effective global institutions be built.

Stories of technology

Technological change regularly impacts on the foreign and defence policies of states, as a result of the need for raw materials or innovations in military strategy. Technology reordered the system after 1945 by making even the most powerful states vulnerable to catastrophic atomic destruction. Such a radical change is not expected in future, but the acceleration of technological innovation should not be underestimated. Who could have guessed what changes the silicone chip would make within a generation?

Looking to the future, power, and therefore international relations, would be transformed by the discovery of cheap and superabundant energy. And what would be the impact of the use of robots and cyborgs to perform hitherto costly, dangerous or impossible tasks? Humanity's capacity for inventing new technologies, as opposed to being able to reinvent itself, is stupendous.

Stories of the unexpected

Surprise has been a regular in the history of international relations, and the capacity of experts for successful prediction remains poor. Unexpected events have often blown away the hopes of leaders and their followers in the past. Do not assume today that we are wiser than in the past, or that things must get better: recall that the glory that was Rome was followed by the 'Dark Ages'. But surprise does not always take the form of bad outcomes. The Cold War ended not with a nuclear bang, but with cheering crowds in the streets; and apartheid wound down in South Africa in a spirit of reconciliation, not the widely predicted 'race war'. Human agency can deliver positive change as well as the opposite.

▶ Three scenarios

As these key stories unfold, the overall structure of international relations will take various trajectories towards 2050. Three scenarios follow, moving from a decentralized to a more centralized world system. Short of a global catastrophe (a world war or radical environmental collapse), the likelihood is that each model will be in play to some degree, though different parts of the world will move at different rates, and not always in the same direction.

Stressed statism

This scenario assumes business as usual. States will remain the basic units of political decision-making and loyalty, but will become increasingly stressed because of competition over security, prosperity and identity in the shrinking global neighbourhood. As a result, the Westphalian state will muddle on while being hollowed out by globalization and other developments. International relations as usual might be dominated by a 'Pax Americana', a 'Pax Sinica', a bipolar confrontation between the two, or a multipolar system.

Alongside this traditional scenario is the prospect of old-time disorder, as sovereign units struggle for security and resources, and the familiar problems of collective decision-making remain unresolved. Confronted by the converging global challenges of the Great Reckoning, this scenario would test the age of Westphalia to breaking point.

The collective action problem

Sustained co-operation remains statecraft's biggest challenge. As ever, nations and their leaders will be confronted by the temptation of immediate selfish gains against the benefits of long-term common endeavour; and for the foreseeable future, acting together to mitigate climate change will be a supreme test. As with disarmament negotiations historically, when governments get together they use fine words but, in practice, favour the so-called national interest, worry about the next election rather than the next generation, drag their feet, have an eye to coming out of whatever negotiations with relative gains, and move at the speed of the slowest major power.

Rampant regionalism

This scenario envisages international relations becoming increasingly focused on continental-sized regions. Institution-building would intensify across continents, and centralized decision-making would become more normal. These regions would concentrate upon economic growth (as is presently the case in South East Asia and the Americas) but possibly also upon political development (as in Europe). But the condition of the EU today is a reminder that success can breed complacency, and that progress in integrative experiments cannot be guaranteed. Moreover, if they are successful, the question arises of how regional power blocs would relate to other regional powers or major states. Will the traditional anarchy imperative simply operate among larger units? Might the outcome become continental-sized opponents wrapped in Cold

War confrontations? Would global regionalism make the 'Clash of Civilizations' real, or might it be a step towards the 'Alliance of Civilizations' advanced by the Prime Ministers of Turkey and Spain in 2005, or even be the arch-stone for a much more centralized global structure of politics among nations?

Global government

This final scenario envisages a system in which authoritative decisions are increasingly collective. Global governance would steadily evolve into *government*, that is, backed by law and ultimately by force. It is important to distinguish here between this picture of a centralizing global polity and the propagandistic term 'international community' used in particular by Tony Blair and George W. Bush to attempt to legitimize (even illegal) acts of 'humanitarian intervention', the war against Iraq and, generally, any controversial policy initiatives.

The ultimate expression of centralized global power would be world government. The most discussed version of this possibility in the past has been a federal model, comprising checks and balances, and the centre's sovereign responsibility restricted to truly global issues. Whatever its form, the idea of world government is generally regarded these days as either fanciful or a nightmare, and it has fallen out of fashionable discussion since the 1950s. Those wanting to be taken seriously by policy-makers or the media avoid the topic, for fear it would damage their reputation for seriousness. Given the growing convergence of global challenges and a shrinking planet, this will surely not always be the case.

▶ One world: we all matter

It is not only state leaders who face tough choices in the biggest political arena. The rest of us, all children of international relations, must decide whether to consign to future generations a world that is not working for thousands of millions of people or the natural world on which we all ultimately depend. Many will reply fatalistically ('What will be will be') or with caution ('Better the devil you know') or with narcissistic nationalism ('My country right or wrong'). These responses should be rejected. We have other choices, albeit within structures resistant to change and possessing limited power as individuals. In solidarity, however, people can create new political realities. We always have.

Immanuel Kant (1724–1804)

Kant, more than other political philosophers, recognized the importance of international relations, offered a comprehensive theoretical picture, and transcended traditional limits of thought. Practical politics have yet to catch up with him. Over two centuries ago he observed that 'a violation of rights in one place is felt throughout the world', and in his classic essay 'Perpetual Peace' (1795)) he was not dreamily utopian: he looked towards the reconstruction of the states system, not its abolition, and, though he hated war, he was not a pacifist. He thought it rational to hope for a better world, but knew the difficulties facing anything in the hands of the 'crooked timber' of humanity. At the centre of Kant's thinking about international relations was the harmony of morality and politics, order through justice, the unity of right and law, the need to think universally, and the openness of human potential through thought. He called on us to dare to know, dare to challenge, and dare to hope.

By emphasizing the multi-level dimensions of international relations and the need for change, this book has echoed Kantian perspectives. Simply put: our global community of fate will not get much right until we get international relations right, for the international level will continue to shape, for better or for worse, the impact of global threats, the opportunities for personal flourishing, and the future of nature.

Arguing the world begins at home. Even if what individuals can do appears trifling, engaging with big issues can recover personal hope and a sense of empowerment. With a clear-eyed view of how and why international relations matter, and an appreciation that there are no quick fixes, an attempt to try and change oneself and others – job by job and meeting by meeting – encourages hope that other worlds are possible. There is much theory in the study of international relations, but it is ultimately a practical activity.

Many of the questions that animated students of this discipline nearly a century ago are still being asked: about peace and war, about justice in a statist world, about the inability of international organizations like the UN to work better, about the appalling gaps between haves and have-nots, about why some countries are rich and some poor, about our inability to get collective answers in the human interest, about the prospects for global reform, and much else. The most intractable and significant political questions of the day focus on the international level of world politics. They should matter to all of us: international relations are about 'big and important things', without doubt, but they are also about small and important things, like you, me and everyone else.

This 100 ideas section gives ways you can explore the subject in more depth. It's much more than just the usual reading list.

100 IDEAS

Ten indispensable texts for IR castaways on a desert island

1   *The Landmark Thucydides: A Comprehensive Guide to the Peloponnesian War* (New York: Touchstone, 1996, edited by Robert B. Strasser).

2   Niccolò Machiavelli, *The Prince* (London: Penguin Books, 1973 [1532]).

3   Thomas Hobbes, *Leviathan* (London: Penguin Books, 1988 [1651]).

4   Immanuel Kant, 'Perpetual Peace' (1795), in *Kant's Political Writings*, edited by Hans Reiss (Cambridge: Cambridge University Press, 1970).

5   Karl von Clausewitz, *On War*, edited and translated by M.E. Howard and Peter Paret (Princeton NJ: Princeton University Press, 1976, [1832]).

6 E.H. Carr, *The Twenty Years' Crisis, 1919–1939: An Introduction to the Study of International Relations* (London: Macmillan, 1946 [1939]).

7 Inis L. Claude, *Swords into Ploughshares: The Problems and Progress of International Organization* (London: University of London Press, 1964 [1956]).

8 Kenneth N. Waltz, *Man, the State and War: A Theoretical Analysis* (New York: Columbia University Press, 1959).

9 Arnold Wolfers, *Discord and Collaboration: Essays on International Politics* (Baltimore: The Johns Hopkins Press, 1962).

10 Hedley Bull, *The Anarchical Society: A Study of Order in World Politics* (London: Macmillan, 1977).

Ten films with insights into international relations

11 Common humanity, the futility of war, class: *The Grand Illusion* (1937), directed by Jean Renoir.

12 Politics and conformity, states and situational ethics, the internationalizing of human rights: *Judgement at Nuremburg* (1961), directed by Stanley Kramer.

13 State of nature, logics of anarchy, power disparities: *Lord of the Flies* (1963), directed by Peter Brook.

14 Nationalist paranoia, macho militarism, nuclear MADness: *Dr Strangelove* (1964), directed by Stanley Kubrick.

15 Ethics of responsibility, technological dangers, nuclear scorpions in a bottle: *Fail-Safe* (1964), directed by Sidney Lumet.

16 Naked (and legitimized) power, strategizing, realpolitik, instrumental violence: *The Godfather I/II/III* (1972, 1974, 1990), directed by Francis Ford Coppola.

17 Decision-making dynamics, the human capacity for radical brutality, euphemistic language: *Conspiracy* (2001), directed by Frank Pierson.

18 Butchers/butchered, sacrifice/sacrificed, heroes/heroized: *Flags of Our Fathers / Letters from Iwo Jima* (2006), directed by Clint Eastwood.

19 Cultural misunderstandings, power and powerlessness, 'stuff happens!': *California Dreamin'* (2007), directed by Cristian Nemescu.

20 Bureaucratic infighting, spin, incompetence: *In the Loop* (2009), directed by Armando Iannucci.

Ten books (in order of first publication) for a comprehensive student starter-pack

21 Kenneth N. Waltz, *Theory of International Politics* (New York: Random House, 1979).

22 Richard A. Falk and Samuel S. Kim, eds, *The War System: An Interdisciplinary Approach* (Boulder: Westview, 1980).

23 Evan Luard, ed., *Basic Texts in International Relations: The Evolution of Ideas about International Society* (Houndmills: Macmillan, 1992).

24 Chris Brown and Kirsten Ainley, *Understanding International Relations* (Houndmills: Palgrave Macmillan, 2009 [1997]).

25 Walter C. Opello and Stephen J. Rosow, *The Nation-State and Global Order: A Historical Introduction to Contemporary Politics* (Boulder: Lynne Rienner, 2004).

26 Anthony Best, Jussi M. Hanhimäki, Joseph A. Maiolo and Kirsten E. Schulze, *International History of the Twentieth Century and Beyond* (London: Routledge, 2004).

27 Joshua S. Goldstein and Jon C. Pevenhouse, *International Relations* (New York: Longman, 2010 [2006]).

28 Tim Dunne, Milja Kurki and Steve Smith, eds, *International Relations Theories: Discipline and Diversity* (Oxford: Oxford University Press, 2013 [2007]).

29 Ken Booth and Nicholas J. Wheeler, *The Security Dilemma: Fear, Cooperation and Trust in World Politics* (Houndmills: Palgrave Macmillan, 2008).

30 William E. Scheuerman, *The Realist Case for Global Reform* (Cambridge: Polity, 2011).

Five pictures of continuities in international relations

31 'Here, then, is the complexity, the fascination and the tragedy of all political life. Politics are made up of two elements – utopia and reality – belonging to two different planes which can never meet.' E.H. Carr, *The Twenty Years' Crisis, 1919–1939: An Introduction to the Study of International Relations* (1946 [1939]).

32 'Politics, like society in general, is governed by objective laws that have their roots in human nature.' Hans J. Morgenthau, *Politics among Nations* (1964 [1948]).

33 'The factors that distinguish international politics ... are (1) that the stakes of the game are considered to be of unusual importance and (2) that in international politics the use of force is not excluded as a means of influencing the outcome. The cardinal rule of the game is often taken to be: Do what you must in order to win it.' Kenneth N. Waltz, *Man, the State and War* (1959).

34 'The great nations have always acted like gangsters, and the small nations like prostitutes.' Stanley Kubrick, *Guardian* (1963).

35 'Strength ensures safety, and the greatest strength is the greatest insurance of safety. States facing this incentive are fated to clash as each competes for advantage over the others. This is a tragic situation, but there is no escaping it unless the states that make up the system agree to form a world government. Such a vast transformation is hardly a realistic prospect, however, so conflict and war are bound to continue as large and enduring features of world politics.' John J. Mearsheimer, *The Tragedy of Great Power Politics* (2001).

Five perspectives on change in history and historians

36 'History, in Burckhardt's words, is "the record of what one age finds worthy or not in another". The past is intelligible to us only in the light of the present; and we can fully understand the present only in the light of the past.' E.H. Carr, *What is History?* (1961).

37 'Men make their own history, but they do not make it just as they please; they do not make it under circumstances chosen by themselves.' Karl Marx, *The Eighteenth Brumaire of Louis Bonaparte* (1852).

38 'Man can change reality, and the necessary conditions for such change already exist.' Max Horkheimer, 'Traditional and Critical Theory' (1937).

39 'Experience and history teaches us this: that people and governments have learnt nothing from history, nor acted on principles deduced from it.' George Wilhelm Hegel, *The Philosophy of History* (1807).

40 'All that is solid melts into air.' Karl Marx and Friedrich Engels, *The Communist Manifesto* (1848).

Ten views on the workings of power

41 'Violence, being instrumental by nature, is rational to the extent that it is effective in reaching the end which must justify it.' Hannah Arendt, 'Reflections on Violence', *New York Review of Books*, 20 July 2013 [1969].

42 'If everyone's strategy depends upon everyone else's, then the Hitlers determine in part the action, or better, reaction, of those whose ends are worthy and whose means are fastidious ... Each state pursues its own interests, however defined, in ways it judges best. Force is a means of achieving the external ends of states because there exists no consistent, reliable process of reconciling the conflicts of interest that inevitably arise among similar units in a condition of anarchy.' Kenneth N. Waltz, *Man, the State and War* (1959).

43 'The chief function of the balance of power ... is not to preserve peace, but to preserve the system of states itself.' Hedley Bull, *The Anarchical Society* (1977).

44 'If this phrase of the "balance of power" is to be always an argument for war, the pretext for war will never be wanting, and peace can be never secure ... This whole notion of the "balance of power" is a mischievous delusion which has come down to us from past times; we ought to drive it from our minds, and to consider the solemn question of peace and war in more clear, more definite, and on far higher principle than any that are involved in the phrase.' John Bright, UK House of Commons, 1854.

45 'Underestimating the amounts and kinds of power operating in the world is the hallmark of *non*feminist analysis.' Cynthia Enloe, *Bananas, Beaches, and Bases: Making Feminist Sense of International Politics* (1989).

46 'Power is where power goes.' Lyndon B. Johnson, 1960.

47 'The aide said that guys like me were "in what we call the reality-based community," which he defined as people who "believe that solutions emerge from your judicious study of discernible reality." ... "That's not the way the world really works anymore," he continued. "We're an empire now, and when we act, we create our own reality. And while you're studying that reality—judiciously, as you will—we'll act again, creating other new realities, which you can study too, and that's how things will sort out. We're history's actors ... and you, all of you, will be left to just study what we do.' Ron Suskind, *New York Times Magazine*, 17 October 2004, quoting an aide (allegedly Karl Rove) of George W. Bush.

48 'Pure realism can offer nothing but a naked struggle for power which makes any kind of international society impossible.' E.H. Carr, *The Twenty Years' Crisis, 1919–1939.*

49 'I am not only a pacifist but a militant pacifist. I am willing to fight for peace. Nothing will end war unless the people themselves refuse to go to war.' Albert Einstein, interview in January 1931.

50 'The practice of violence, like all action, changes the world, but the most probable change is a more violent world.' Hannah Arendt, 'Reflections on Violence' (2013 [1969]).

Ten debating points about states, nations and nationalism

51 'Our object in the construction of the state is the greatest happiness of the whole, and not that of any one class.' Plato (*c.* 380 BCE).

52 'The state exists for the sake of a good life, and not for the sake of life only.' Aristotle (350 BCE).

53 'Who saves his country violates no law.' Napoleon I (Emperor of the French 1804–15).

54 'The state? What is that? ... The state is the coldest of all cold monsters. Coldly it lies, too ... the state lies in all languages of good and evil; and whatever it says, it lies – and whatever it has, it has stolen.' Friedrich Nietzsche (1883).

55 'No nation is fit to sit in judgement upon any other nation.' Woodrow Wilson (1915).

56 'Patriotism is a lively sense of responsibility. Nationalism is a silly cock crowing on its own dungheap.' Richard Aldington (1931).

57 'Talking of patriotism, what humbug it is; it is a word which always commemorates a robbery. There isn't a foot of land in the world which doesn't represent the ousting and re-ousting of a long line of successive owners.' Mark Twain (1935).

58 'A nation is a society united by a delusion about its ancestry and by a common hatred of its neighbours.' Dean (William Ralph) Inge (1948).

59 'We must free ourselves from thinking in terms of nation states... The countries of Western Europe are no longer in a position to protect themselves individually; not one of them is any longer in a position to salvage Europe's culture.' Konrad Adenauer (1953).

60 'You're not to be so blind with patriotism that you can't face reality. Wrong is wrong, no matter who does it or who says it.' Malcolm X (1965).

Ten places to feel the power of international politics

61 **Wartime sacrifice:** the Piskariovskoye Memorial Cemetery, St Petersburg (Leningrad), Russia.

62 **The start of the nuclear age:** Hiroshima, Japan.

63 **International hopes and frustrations:** UN Building, New York City, United States.

64 **Post-national institutionalization:** European Union complex, Brussels, Belgium.

65 **The largest slum in Africa:** Kibera (Nairobi), Kenya.

66 **A tinderbox:** the Gaza strip, Palestine.

67 **A superpower challenged:** 9/11 Memorial, Lower Manhattan, New York City, United States.

68 **A crossroads of continents:** the waterfront in Istanbul, Turkey.

69 **The hub of a booming economy and rising world power:** Shanghai, People's Republic of China.

70 **Globalization – growth, glitz, pollution and garbage:** Bangalore, India.

Ten word problems and world problems: phrases best avoided

71 'I am proud of my nation' (pure cultural narcissism).

72 'There is no alternative' (there invariably is).

73 'Just war' (wars should not be considered 'just'; at best, they might be considered 'excusable').

74 'Friend' (states and their representatives should not be confused with interpersonal relations).

75 'Internationalism' (a pious euphemism largely devoid of meaning).

76 'Independence' (all states these days are interdependent, and some – the weakest – are most interdependent of all).

77 'International community' (a term that evolved from meaning the collective will of the League of Nations to being a slogan expressing the ethnocentrism of the leading Western powers).

78 'I have always believed...' (arguments do not become truer the longer one holds them).

79 'The national interest' (the favourite we-are-all-in-it-together cover for policies serving particularist perspectives).

80 'Never' (international history is too long and too indeterminate for such a word).

Ten non-governmental information sources for monitoring major trends

81 Dan Smith, *The State of the World Atlas*, 9th edn (Oxford: The New Internationalist, 2013). A reliable, comprehensive and accessible guide.

82 Stuart Casey-Maslen, ed., *The War Report 2012* (Oxford: Oxford University Press, 2013). A new annual report offering overviews of all armed conflicts, including the legal issues they raise.

83 www.un.org (the main UN website, with links to the main organs of the UN such as the Security Council, and access to official documents and reports).

84 http://oneworld.net (provides access to international NGOs – 'helping the world's poorest people to improve their lives', offering ideas about how to 'understand and act on global problems'). See also www.oxfam.org.uk.

85 www.iisd.org (International Institute for Sustainable Development, based in Winnipeg, Canada, with the mission 'to champion innovation, enabling societies to live sustainably').

86 http://www.responsibilitytoprotect.org (New York-based international coalition providing extensive materials on atrocity prevention and protection).

87 www.sipri.org (the Stockholm International Peace Research Institute has provided authoritative and extensive information on conflict, weapons and arms control and disarmament since 1966).

88 www.cris.unu.edu (the United Nations University Institute on Comparative Regional Integration Studies (UNU – CRIS) is a research and training institute of the United Nations University. UNU – CRIS specializes in studying the processes and consequences of regional integration and co-operation).

89 www.amnesty.org and www.hrw.org (Amnesty and Human Rights Watch are the major global human rights NGOs).

90 http://ifg.org (the International Forum on Globalization – based in San Francisco and founded in 1994 – promotes research, advocacy and action to secure democracy and sustainability, locally and globally).

Ten reasons to think a better world is possible

91 Ashoka the Great (304–232 BCE), enlightened Buddhist emperor of India.

92 Mahatma Gandhi (1869–1949), non-violent civil rights leader and philosopher.

93 Nelson Mandela (1918–2013), a political life incredibly well lived.

94 Mordechai Vanunu (1954–), nuclear weapons whistleblower.

95 Malala Yousafzai (1997–), young education activist, brave beyond her years.

96 Those who have sought to make the United Nations more than a club of sovereign states.

97 **Amnesty International** (founded 1961): ordinary people, worldwide, seeking to promote the rights of others, everywhere.

98 **Greenpeace** (started in 1971) and other organizations aspiring to promote global consciousness and citizenship.

99 **The border between Germany and France:** within living memory a battlefield where countless soldiers fought and died over the centuries; today a frontier of free movement.

100 **The knowledge that peace, tolerance and co-operation have existed and still do exist in many places.** A better world is immanent (latent or inherent) in human society, even if not presently imminent (likely to occur soon).

Index

A

Allott, Philip, 49
ambition, 53
anarchy, 3, 46, 74
Asian values of human rights, 105
authorities, 27

B

balance of power, 10, 61
behaviouralism, 38–9
Bell, Daniel, 56
Bentham, Jeremy, 6–7
Bretton Woods system, 89–90

C

Cameron, David, 94
capitalism, 41–2, 88–94, 127–8
change, 119
Churchill, Winston, 71–2
city-states, 19
civilizations, 45
   early, 18–21
Clausewitz, Karl von, 66
climate change, 126–7
Clinton, Bill, 84
Cold War, 5–6, 37
collective actions, 125–7
collective identities, 27
colonialization, 25
communitarianism, 109–10
Concert of Europe, 71
constructivism, 45–6
continuity, 9
co-operation, 70–3, 79–80, 125–6
cosmopolitanism, 110
Cox, Robert W., 42–3
critical theory vs. mainstream theory,
   42–4

Cuban Missile Crisis (1962), 103
cultural relativism, 105–6

D

Davies, David, 10–11
decision-making, 75
   collective, 125–6
   ethics, 101–4
defence, 26–7, 51–2
democratic peace theory
   (DPT), 37–8
diplomacy, 64, 74–9
diversity, 112
dominant states, 122–3

E

economics, 27–8, 84–97, 127–8
Eisenhower, Dwight D., 103
emancipation, 128–9
empires, early, 19–20
ethics of responsibility, 101–4

F

Fail-Safe (2000 film), 100–1
fear, 48–53
Featherstone, Mike, 17
feminism, 43
feudal system, 20–1
financial crises, 93
First World War (1914–18),
   5, 10
foreign policy, 74–9
Foucault, Michel, 57
Francis I, King of France, 9
Frankfurt School, 42–3
Fukuyama, Francis, 44–5, 46
functionalism, 86

G

G-20 (Group of Twenty), 90
Galbraith, Kenneth J., 93
Genghis Khan, 20
Germany, 9–10, 77
global concerns, 112–16
global governance, 132
global regionalism, 131
globalism vs. state-centrism, 40–2
globalization, 94–7
Gorbachev, M. S., 103
Gramsci, Antonio, 57
Great War of Africa (1998–2003), 67
Greece
  city-states, 19
  the Melian Dialogue, 54
green theory, 43

H

hard power vs. soft power,
    57–8, 86
Hardy, Thomas, 64, 73
harmony of interests, 68–9
hegemony, 123
Heilbronner, Robert, 93–4
Herz, John, 51
hierarchy, 122–3
high politics vs. low politics, 87
historic IR canon, 12
Hobbes, Thomas, 50
human nature, 48–50
human rights, 104–8
  emancipation, 128–9
humanity, 119–20, 133–4
Huntington, Samuel P., 45, 46, 110

I

idealism vs. realism, 34–8
identity, 6, 16–17, 108–12, 121–2
  collective, 27
independence, political, 28–9

Indian empires, 20
individualism, 93–4
individuals
  concerns, 4–6
  human rights, 104–8
influence, 57
integration, 70

J

judgement vs. science, 38–40

K

Kahn, Herman, 100
Kant, Immanuel, 133–4
Kennedy, John F., 103
Khrushchev, N. S., 103

L

Louis XIV, King of France, 23–4
low politics vs. high politics, 87

M

mainstream theory vs. critical theory,
    42–4
Melian Dialogue, 54
miniaturization, 115
Mitrany, David, 85–6
Mongol empire, 20
Monnet, Jean, 85
moral dilemmas, 101–4
moral relativism, 106
Mueller, John, 67

N

nation-states, 24–5, 26
national identity, 108–9
national interest, 74–5
nationalism, 24–6
neoliberalism, 91, 92–4
neo-Marxism, 40–2
nuclear co-operation, 72–3

nuclear weapons, 26–7, 51–2
Nye, Joseph S., 56–7

O

Obama, Barack, 75–6
optimism, 118–20

P

Palmerston, Lord, 71
peace, 69–73, 114–15
Pinker, Steven, 67–8
political independence, 28–9
positivism, 38
poststucturalism, 44
poverty, 59
power, 53–8, 86
   global, 132
predictions, 130–2
   difficulties, 77
   surprises, 129–30
Putin, Vladimir, 76

R

rational choice theory, 39–40, 77
realism vs. idealism, 34–8
regionalism, 131
religious identity, 110–12, 122
revolutions, 124–5
Roman empire, 19–20
Rosenau, James, 41
Russia, power, 56 *see also* Soviet
      Union

S

Scheuerman, William E., 35
science vs. judgement, 38–40
Second World War (1939–45), 5
secularism, 111
security, 58–61
   dilemmas, 51–3
security community theory, 70

Sen, Amartya, 111
Smith, Dan, 28
soft power vs. hard power, 57–8, 86
solitarist identity, 111
sovereignty, 22–4, 26, 120–1
   challenges, 26–30
Soviet Union, 87–8, 89 *see also* Russia
stable peace, 69–73
Stalin, Joseph, 56
state-centrism vs. globalism, 40–2
'state of nature', 50–3
state sovereignty, 22–4, 26
   challenges, 26–30
states, 7–8, 130–1
   alternatives, 17
   division, 16–17
   dominant, 122–3
   vs. nations, 24–5
structure, 36
students of International Relations,
      10–13, 32–3, 46
Syria, 102–3

T

Taylor, A. J. P., 10
technological advances, 129
teleology, 16
'texture' of the international, 9–10, 30
Thatcher, Margaret, 85
Thirty Years War (1618–48),
      21–2
Tilly, Charles, 21
transnationalism, 40–1
Truman, Harry S., 103

U

Ukraine crisis, 64–5
United States, 13
   power, 56
Universal Declaration of Human
      Rights (UDHR), 105, 107

V

Voltaire, 16

W

Wallerstein, Immanuel, 41, 88–9
Waltz, Kenneth N., 3–4, 35–6, 65–6

wars, 5–6, 21–2, 64–9, 123–4
    perceived inevitability, 49–51
Weber, Max, 101
Westphalian system, 22–3,
    29, 121
Wotton, Henry, 64